THE 'AFRIC

C. S. FORESTER

Simplified by Michael West

Illustrated by Golden Wesley

1500 word vocabulary

LONGMAN

.

LONGMAN GROUP UK LIMITED
Longman House, Burnt Mill, Harlow
Essex CM20 2JE, England
and Associated Companies throughout the world

*This edition first published by Longman Group Ltd
(formerly Longmans, Green & Co Ltd)
in association with Michael Joseph Ltd 1964
New impressions *1965 (twice); *1966; *1967;
*1969; *1970; *1971; *1972;
*1973; *1974; *1975; *1977;
*1978; *1979 (twice);
*1981 (thrice); *1984;
*1986; *1987;
*1988

Produced by Longman Group (FE) Ltd
Printed in Hong Kong

ISBN 0-582-53495-X

CONTENTS

It was very slow and very difficult paddling the boat through the water (see page 66)

One

ALONE – WITH A DEAD MAN IN AN AFRICAN FOREST

The date of this story is 1914 – in the First World War. The place is a part of Africa then held by the Germans. Rose Sayer and her brother, Samuel Sayer, worked in a *mission*: they were *missionaries*: they had a church and a school and taught Christianity to the Africans in the village.

*   *   *

Rose Sayer could see that her brother Samuel was very ill: he had become worse. He knelt down to say the evening prayer but his hands shook, and his voice was very weak. He prayed God to forgive them and guide them in their lives. Then he began to say his usual prayer for God's blessing upon the mission; but his voice failed. They had given their lives to the mission, but now it had ceased to be. General von Hanneken and his soldiers had carried away all the people from the village to be soldiers or bearers in the Army of German Central Africa. All the animals and food had been taken – everything except the little house in which Samuel and Rose lived.

Then Samuel prayed that God would bless the

armies of England and bring victory. His voice was stronger now: there was a sound of the fighting spirit in it.

"Amen! Amen! Amen!" said Rose.

"I think, sister," said Samuel, "that I will go to bed now."

It was midnight before she fell asleep, but it was sunrise when she awoke. Her brother must have been calling to her. She hurried out of her bedroom and across the living-room into Samuel's room. Samuel must have been calling to her; but he was not able to call now. She could not understand most of what he was saying. "The poor Mission," he said. "It was the Germans."

He died soon after that. Rose wept at his bedside. At last she slowly stood up. The morning sun was pouring down upon the forest and on the empty and deserted place where the village had been. She was alone.

She was alone; but her fear did not last long. She was thirty-three years old and had spent ten years in the Central African forest: she had learned to trust herself. She had her Christian faith to give her strength.

Soon she felt a wild anger against the Germans. Von Hanneken had killed Samuel: he had destroyed the labour of ten years. Worse than that, they had harmed the word of God. None of their followers would ever come back to the mission.

From childhood she had been taught to love and look up to her brother and, when he became a priest, she respected him still more. She had kept house for him, obeyed him, helped him for ten years. It was not surprising that she felt an un-Christian anger against the people who had caused his death.

Her brother had prayed for the success of the British armies and for victory over the Germans. She remembered how she had read in the Bible about 'destroying the Amalakites and the Philistines and the Midianites'. She longed to strike a blow for England and destroy her enemies; but that was day-dreaming. There was no possible chance of her doing anything.

Just at this moment Rose lifted her eyes and saw a man looking out carefully from the trees beyond the village. She did not know that this was her chance; she had no idea that this man would be the instrument which she would use to strike her blow for England. All she saw at that moment was that it was Allnutt, a London working-man employed by the Belgians at the gold mine two hundred miles up the river. Her brother did not like him: he did not behave in a Christian way: he was bad for the Africans.

But it was an English face, a friendly face. She was no longer alone in the forest.

She hurried out and waved her hand to Allnutt.

Two

FIRST DAY ON THE 'AFRICAN QUEEN'

"Where is everyone, Miss?" asked Allnutt.

"They have all gone," said Rose.

"Where is your brother?"

"He's in there. He's dead." She must not show her grief: that would be weakness. She shut her mouth in its usual firm line.

"Dead? That's bad. Have the Germans been here Miss?"

"Yes," said Rose. "Look."

He saw the ring of empty huts, – no men, no women, no children, and the silent forest beyond.

"Bad, isn't it, Miss! Up at the mine it was just the same," said Allnutt. "They have taken everything. I don't know what they have done with the Belgians. I wouldn't like to be a prisoner of that tall fellow – Hanneken. All my men ran away in the night and left me with the *launch*." [a small ship].

"The launch?" said Rose, sharply.

"Yes, Miss. The 'African Queen'. I went up the river to Limbasi for stores. They didn't think that the Germans would fight: they just gave me the stuff and let me go. I suppose Hanneken has done the same to them as he did to the mine. But he hasn't got the launch nor what's in her. He would be glad to have it!"

"What's in it?" asked Rose.

"Blasting Gelatine, Miss: that's an explosive which they use in the mine. Eight boxes of it. And *cylinders* – steel cases – of gas. They use that to get great heat for joining pieces of metal together. Hanneken would find a use for all that."

They went into the house.

"How long has he been dead, Miss?"

"He died this morning."

In hot countries you can't leave a dead man for more than six hours.

"All right, Miss," said Allnutt. "I'll dig a grave."

"I have my prayer book," said Rose. "I can read the service."

Allnutt looked round the edge of the forest to see if there were any Germans. Then he looked for a place for the grave.

"Just here would be the best place," he said, pointing. "The ground won't be too hard, and I think he would like to be in the shade. – We had better be quick, miss. The Germans may come back again."

When it was all finished, Rose stood in sorrow beside the grave. Allnutt waited: he moved about beside her, wanting to go.

"Come on down the river, Miss. Let's get away from here."

Rose put her few possessions in a bag and they started out together.

There was a steep path through the forest to the river. In some places the ground was very soft and they went into it up to their knees. Sometimes the

Rose stood in sorrow beside the grave

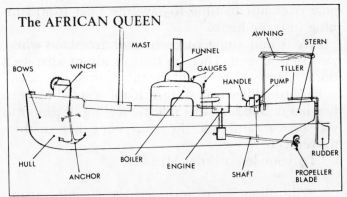

A Plan of the 'African Queen'

roots of trees helped them. At every step the smell of the river became stronger. Then they came out from the forest into the blinding sunshine. The launch lay there, close to the water's edge. The brown water of the river rushed past her.

"Careful now, Miss," said Allnutt. "Put your foot here, on this root. That's right."

Rose sat in the launch and looked about her. This launch was very important to her. It was about thirty feet long. The paint was coming off. The *bows* (front of the ship) were heaped high with boxes. There was an *awning* at the *stern* to keep off the heat and the sun; but Rose could feel the heat of the boiler as she sat there in the shadow.

Allnutt put more wood on the fire. Smoke came out of the *funnel*. The *engine* began to move. He pulled up the *anchor*. The *propeller* began to turn faster and Allnutt pushed out the launch from the bank. Then he pushed Rose aside as he put the *tiller* over just in time to save the boat from running into the bank.

"We'll find some place behind an island where we can't be seen. Then we can talk about what we'll do. . . . Here, Miss! Hold the tiller just as it is now."

The iron tiller was so hot that it seemed to burn her hand. She had a wonderful feeling of power as she *steered*[1] and felt the ship obey her smallest movement.

"To your left a little, Miss."

The boat went into a narrow side-stream. Allnutt came jumping over the boxes of explosive and shut off the engine. Then he ran forward again and let go the anchor. The 'African Queen' stopped. The branches of the trees met above them, and below they sat in a green light. There was silence. The only sound to be heard was the rush of the water. It was cool – wonderfully cool. And then the flies and other biting *insects* came out with a rush from the bushes. They came in clouds, biting them without mercy.

Allnutt came back to the stern where Rose sat under the awning in the stern. He had a cigarette hanging from his mouth. He had a thin beard. He still seemed afraid as he battled with the insects, but he tried to hide his fear.

"Well, here we are, Miss; safe. The question is what next?"

"We've got plenty of food. Two thousand cigarettes. Two cases of *gin*.[2] We can stay here for

[1] *To steer* = to guide.
[2] *Gin* = a strong drink: usually drunk with water.

THE LOUISA

months if we want to. How long do you think the war will last?"

Rose looked at him in silence. Allnutt wanted them to remain here until the war was ended! He had no idea of striking a blow for England!

"We don't know which way help will come," said Allnutt. "They might come up the railway to Limbasi and we could go there. One thing is certain: they won't come across the Lake and up this river. Nothing can cross the Lake while the 'Louisa' is there."

The 'Louisa' was a German police-boat with a six-pounder gun (a gun throwing a shot weighing six pounds).

The 'Louisa' had been brought up from the coast in pieces and put together at the Lake eight years ago. Rose could remember this. Roads had to be cut through the forest and hundreds of Africans helped to carry it. Then the 'Louisa' kept order on the Lake and the land round it, stopped thieves from stealing the boats, and stopped Africans fighting one another. Fields and villages began to spread along the side. But now the 'Louisa' ruled the Lake as firmly as Britain ruled the seas around her shore.

"Hanneken wouldn't last a month without the 'Louisa'," said Allnutt: "the British could get at him across the Lake. But, as it is he might hold out against them for ever."

He went on smoking his cigarette.

Then he said, "All this doesn't get us nearer home, does it, Miss? I can't think what we can do."

"We must do something for England!" said Rose.

"Coo!" said Allnutt: – that was his usual cry of surprise. "Coo!"

Allnutt's idea was to be as far away from the war as possible; but he saw the light in Rose's face, and felt he must say the right thing to her.

"Yes, Miss," he said. "If there was anything we could do, I'd be the first to say we ought to do it. – What is your idea?"

"This river, the Ulanga, runs into the Lake, doesn't it?"

"Yes, Miss; but if you were thinking of going down the river into the Lake. . . . Well, you needn't think about it! We can't!"

"Why not?"

"Because of the rapids, Miss. Those are places where the river flows very fast over rocks and through narrow places. No one has ever gone down that part of the river, except a man named Spengler."

"He got down it: I remember."

"Yes, Miss, in an African boat with six men. There are places where the river is only twenty yards wide and the water rushes down. You might get down this in a little boat, but you'd never get this launch through."

"Then how did the launch reach here?"

"By rail, Miss, like all other heavy stuff. I think

they sent the pieces up to Limbasi and put them together on the bank. The 'Louisa' was carried to the Lake on men's backs."

"Yes, I remember," said Rose. Samuel had got into trouble at that time because he spoke out against the way the Africans were treated in doing this. Now her brother was dead, and he had been the best man on earth. She had stood by his side in his endless quarrels with the Germans. Under his orders she had tried to learn Swahili and German and other languages. Women of her class did what their men ordered.

Now she had to make her own judgment of a man's character. That wasn't easy. She looked for a long time at Allnutt's face, with a cloud of insects round it.

She came out to this place ten years ago with her brother. As the ship passed through Gibraltar, Malta, Port Said, she saw the British battleships and was proud of Britain's place in the world. But her brother was a man of peace; he thought it wrong to spend money on battleships; it would be better to spend it on feeding the poor and teaching Christianity in other lands. Now her brother was dead, and those early thoughts came back to her. He said that the war would never come; but it had come. Britain was in danger.

She stood up in the stern of the launch and went past the engine to the place where the stores were heaped up in the bow.

"What are these boxes with red lines on them?"

"That's the explosive – Blasting Gelatine: I told you about it. . . . It's quite safe. It won't explode if you hit it, or set fire to it. It will only explode if you use a *detonator*: that is if you explode something else into it. – But I'll put it over the side if you're afraid of it."

"No!" said Rose. "We may want it."

Rose pointed to the cylinders of gas. "Those are the cylinders?"

"Yes, Miss. Cylinders of gas. We can't find any use for them. I'll drop them over the side."

"No! Don't do that!" Rose remembered something: she looked at the cylinders again. "They look like *torpedoes*, those things which warships send under water to blow up another ship. – Allnutt, could you make a torpedo?"

Allnutt laughed. "Could I make a torpedo! Ask me to build a battleship! You don't know what you're saying. A torpedo has an engine in it, and an instrument which makes it run straight in the right direction and at the right depth. A torpedo costs a thousand pounds to make."

"But all these things," said Rose, "only make the thing go. We can put the explosive inside the cylinders: they can be pushed out in front of the launch. Then we can run the launch against the side of a ship, and they'll explode, – just like a torpedo."

"Yes," said Allnutt, "but I don't know what we would want to torpedo as this is the only boat on the river; but supposing we did that, supposing we did torpedo something, what would happen to us? It would blow up this launch and us and everything. Think again, Miss!"

Rose knew quite well what she wanted to torpedo, and did not mind being blown up. If she died striking a blow for England she would certainly go to heaven and have a golden crown. But the hope of heaven and a golden crown would not lead Allnutt to run into danger of being blown up, and, from what she knew of his earlier life and what Samuel had said of him, it was not at all sure that he would go to heaven. She must think of some answer to that.

"We wouldn't be in the launch. We would get everything ready and then point the launch at the other ship and send it away."

"Well. . . .," said Allnutt, "it might work. We could cut holes in the bow of the ship and push the cylinders through them as low down, near the water, as possible. I could make detonators."

"All right," said Rose. "We'll go down to the Lake and torpedo the 'Louisa'."

"Don't be silly, Miss. We can't do that. I told you that. We really can't. We can't get down the river."

"Spengler did."

"In a little boat, Miss."

"That just shows that we can do it, too."

Rose's idea seemed the dream of a mad woman to Allnutt. The one part of the plan which was at all real was the making of the torpedoes. He could make detonators and two cylinders full of explosive would certainly put an end to any other ship. But he did not believe that they could possibly go down the Ulanga river and so there was no chance of using them.

What he expected was that after going over one or two of the smaller rapids, Rose would see what a silly idea it was to go over a big one and they could settle down comfortably and wait for something else to help them. Or perhaps the 'African Queen' would be lost – without loss of life! – Or her engine, which was very old, might break down in a way which he could not repair.

"Well," he thought, "there are two hundred miles of quiet river before the rapids begin and there's no need to trouble myself about next week till next week comes."

"As you wish, Miss," he said. "But don't blame me."

He sat down beside the engine and lit another cigarette. Then he saw Rose's feet. He looked up and saw her standing opposite him as if expecting something. He looked up at her face.

"Come on!" she said. "Aren't we going to start?"

"What, now, Miss?"

"Yes! Now! Come along."

"There are only two hours of daylight left, Miss."

"We can go a long way in two hours," said Rose.

"I'll have to heat up the boiler again," said Allnutt.

He put wood on the fire. He pulled up the anchor and got the propeller turning. Rose watched him. She wanted to learn all about this boat.

She took the tiller and began to learn how to steer the launch. She had to steer the launch through narrow streams among the islands. In some places the water was not deep enough and

she had to keep away from them. There were dead
trees in the water, and plants which might get
mixed up with the propeller. She looked forward
with narrowed eyes over the water. At last they came
to the open river.

Allnutt was very busy with the engine. It was
very old and had been treated very badly. Steam
came out from badly-made joints. He put more
wood on the fire and watched the steam pressure
in the boiler. He ran from point to point oiling
the moving parts. It was wonderful that he had
been able to bring the launch down from Limbasi
to the mission without any of his Africans, his
helpers, doing all this and steering the launch too.

"We must get some more wood," said Allnutt.
"We'll have to stop and anchor soon."

Rose saw that the sun was below the tree-tops.
"All right," she said, unwillingly. "We'll find somewhere to spend the night."

"Round here, Miss!"

Rose put the tiller over and they went up a narrow
channel – a side-stream leading into the big river.

"Round here again! –Bring her in here."

The channel was roofed over with trees and
the bank was made by their roots washed clean by
the brown water of the stream.

Allnutt let go the anchor in the bow of the launch.
Then he ran back and shut off the steam. Rose
understood why it was necessary that the launch
should have its bow pointing up stream: she could
imagine what would happen to a boat if it lay across
that narrow water-way: the water would come over

the side and fill it.

Allnutt came and sat down.

"Coo! It's hot work, isn't it, Miss? I need a drink."

He produced a large dirty cup and then a second one.

"Will you have a drink, Miss?"

"No!" said Rose. She knew what she was going to meet – the 'Evil of Drink' as Samuel always called it. Allnutt pulled out a box from under the seat: he took out of it a bottle of clear liquid, like water.

"What is it?" asked Rose.

"Gin, Miss."

Samuel had always fought against Drink: "It makes men become mad. It destroys them, body and mind. It is the cause of all evil." That was what Samuel used to say.

Allnutt filled one cup with river-water, then poured a little dirty water into the gin in the other cup. Rose watched him. She wanted to stop him, to beg him not to do it. She wanted even to take this evil thing away from him. Allnutt drank the stuff and seemed to enjoy it.

"That's better!" he said. He put the cup down. Rose expected him to begin singing songs or behaving like a madman. But he didn't. All he said was: "Now I can think about supper. Would you like a cup of tea, Miss?"

A cup of tea! The thought of it filled her with excitement. She and Samuel used to drink twelve cups of tea each, every day. Today she had had no tea, – and she had not eaten any food; but food did

not matter. Tea! A cup of tea! Two cups of tea! Six cups of strong tea bringing back life into her tired body.

"Yes, I would like a cup of tea," she said.

"The water is still boiling in the engine. It won't take a minute."

The tinned meat was liquid with the heat. The African bread was black and unpleasant; but the tea was wonderful. Rose had to put tinned milk in it, which she hated: at the mission they had cows. But she drank it, strong, cup after cup; and, as she drank she felt life and comfort coming back to her.

"Those Belgians up at the mine wouldn't ever drink tea," said Allnutt, pouring more milk out of the tin into the black liquid in his cup. "They didn't know what was good for them."

"Yes," said Rose, driving away the flies: they no longer made her feel angry.

Allnutt washed the cups and plates. Then he said, rather doubtfully, "I want to have a bath before bed-time."

"So do I."

"Well, I'll go up to the bow of the boat. You stay down here and do what you like, Miss."

Allnutt went up to the bow, and after a short time Rose heard him having his bath.

She sat on the side of the boat and lowered her legs into the water. The fast stream, wonderfully cool, pulled at her feet. She went over the side and, holding onto the boat, lay at her full length in the water. It was like heaven! So much better than her bath at the mission, in a small iron bath with warm water and afraid all the time that the village children might be looking at her through a hole in the wall.

Then she began to pull herself out; it wasn't easy because of the pull of the stream, but at last she was able to draw herself up and fall inwards over the edge. "Oh!" She thought, "I had quite calmly thought of calling to Allnutt to help me . . . How could I!"

"Are you ready, Miss?" called Allnutt.

"Yes."

He came. "You can sleep here, in the stern."

"Where are you going to sleep?"

"I'll make a bed on those cases in the bows."

"What! On the explosives?"

"Yes: it won't do any harm . . . You can pull these warm coverings over you: it gets very cold on the river towards morning."

She lay down and closed her eyes, but still seemed to see running water. She thought of Allnutt, sleeping only a few yards away; then of the dead Samuel. She thought of the sunlight and shadow on the water when they first anchored.

And then she fell asleep.

Three

RAIN

Rose slept most of the night. Then the storm woke her up. All round her there was a fearful noise – a terrible noise. The rain was pouring down as it can only in Central Africa. A warm wind blew the rain under the awning. Then the water began to come through the awning: little waterfalls came down onto the floor round her. She saw something moving in the launch: Allnutt was coming on hands and knees pulling his bed-clothes along with him. He came up beside her. The awning poured a mass of water down his neck.

"Coo!" he said, and moved to another place. He kept moving from place to place but the streams of water found him every time. He was shaking with cold as he came near her and she almost put out her arm to draw him to her like a child; then she was ashamed of discovering such a thought in her mind, for Allnutt was no more a child than she was.

She sat up and asked, "What can we do?"

"N-nothing, Miss," said Allnutt. "But this won't last long."

He moved from one stream of water into another. Samuel would have been angry in such a state; but Allnutt in his hard life had learned to suffer silently.

"You poor man!" said Rose. "I'm so sorry!" but Allnutt only moved uncomfortably again.

The storm passed as quickly as it came. The wind died away. Day came with a rush. For once they were glad of the heat of the sun. Steam rose up from the water all around them.

"What must be done before we move on?" asked Rose.

"We must get some wood; and then we've got to *pump* out the water from the boat."

"Show me how to do that," said Rose.

"Push the foot of the pump down between the side of the boat and the floor," said Allnutt.

"Work the *handle* up and down. Then the water below the floor is drawn up and sent over the side."

"You go and get wood," said Rose. "I'll do this by myself."

But the pump was old and as difficult to work as everything else on the launch. Sometimes it was stopped up with dirt and no water came: sometimes it stuck and the handle would not move. That pump was a devil! Rose hated it more than she had hated anything before. Her face became redder and redder as she worked away with the devilish thing.

After some time Allnutt appeared on the bank and threw down a heap of dead wood. Then he came with another load, and another. Then he began to put it into the launch. Rose left the pump and helped him. Then he went to get more wood, and Rose started pumping again.

At last there was very little water below the floor. When the wood had all been got into the launch, they stopped and looked at each other.

"We had better start now," said Rose.

"Breakfast? . . . Tea?" said Allnutt hopefully.

"We can have that as we go along," said Rose. "Lets get started now."

"She is a bit mad," he thought, "but it is more trouble to talk to her and make her change her mind than to obey her – at present." So he set himself to get the fire going again under the boiler; then he continued the endless task of oiling the engine.

Rose was interested to see how Allnutt meant to get the launch out from the narrow channel in which she was anchored.

First he tried to pull up the anchor; but the stream was running too fast: so he started the propeller turning until the pull on the anchor-chain was less. Then he got the anchor in. Then he hurried back to the engine and made the propeller go more slowly so that the launch was being carried gently down by the stream although the engine was still driving it forwards.

Rose could not steer the launch when it was going backwards. Allnutt came and took the tiller. When they had just reached the river he ran back to the engine and got the propeller going the other way, – pulling the launch backwards. He rushed back to the tiller and made the stern go up-stream in the river: he then ran back and started the propeller in the opposite direction, then ran back to the tiller to steer the boat down-stream.

Rose could understand how very well Allnutt had

done this. She smiled; but Allnutt gave the tiller to Rose and ran back to the engine which was giving trouble.

When the engine was going well he was able to prepare breakfast. He brought Rose's breakfast to her and she did not even notice the dirty oiliness of his hands. She ate and drank as she held the tiller, and was almost happy.

Rose was learning things about the movement of water, the signs where it was deep, or where there were rocks. She did not know what a fine picture she made, sun-burned, with a firm mouth and narrowed eyes as she stood at the tiller in the bright sunlight.

The heat became greater as the sun rose higher. The river became wider, half a mile across. Von Hanneken and his army were somewhere over there on the other bank. His men were watching the river. Allnutt stood up looking anxiously at the bank.

Rose understood: she turned the 'African Queen' across to the far side where a long narrow island could be seen. They left the sunlight and went into the blessed shade. The water behind the launch began to break in long waves against the bank. The water-plants close to the side bowed their heads as the boat came near and passed them.

Then the stream broke into three channels and Rose had to decide quickly which one to follow.

These side-streams among the islands were silent places. Even the birds were silent in that steaming heat. It seemed as if the noise of the 'African

Queen's' engine was the first sound ever heard there. Rose found herself speaking in whispers.

The first day was very like all the days which they spent going down the river until they came to the rapids. Sometimes they were stopped by trees growing across the water, so that they had to go back and find some other way round.

Sometimes the stream was full of water-plants which were turned round the propeller, and Allnutt had to take off his clothes and go and cut them away: then they had to push the boat forward with the boat *hook*.[1] Each time it was pushed into the *mud*[2] at the bottom, gas came up from the decaying plants so that the place smelt. Sometimes storms came: the rain poured down, and the water came above the floor and Rose had to work long and painfully with that devilish instrument – the pump. Rose was thankful that it was not the Spring when the storms were much longer and heavier than these. These little daily storms were nothing!

Rose was really alive for the first time in her life. She did not know it in her mind; but her body told her. She had passed ten years in that mission, but she had not lived during those years. She had never read any books which told her what a wonderful and exciting place Central Africa was. Samuel had taken no interest in anything except the mission. He knew nothing else – nothing about the plants and animals and birds and insects, – nothing. When von Hanneken destroyed the mission he had nothing else to live for.

[1] *Hook* = piece of bent metal. [2] *Mud* = very wet, soft earth.

It was different now! This plan of going to the Lake and freeing it from the Germans was enough to keep anyone happy! And every day there was the river, with its dangers and difficulties, always changing. These few days of active happiness repaid Rose for thirty-three years of suffering.

Four

GIN

An evening came when Allnutt was silent as if suffering from some secret grief. There was no feeling of companionship as they drank their tea. When the tea was drunk, Allnutt got out the gin bottle and poured a drink for himself, the second drink that day. Then, still silent, he filled his cup again. He drank again, his third drink, and the drink seemed to make him worse.

Rose watched him. She must do something to keep up the spirits of her helper. There was trouble coming, and this silent drinking would only make it worse.

"What's the matter, Allnutt?" she asked gently.

Allnutt only drank again and looked down at his feet. Rose came across, nearer to him.

"Tell me," she said. Then Allnutt answered: "We're not going any further down the river. We've gone far enough. This idea of going to the Lake is silly."

"Not going any further!" she said. "Allnutt! Of course we must! What's the matter?"

"The river is the matter. And Shona. If we go on tomorrow, we'll be in the rapids tomorrow night. But before we get to the rapids we'll have to pass Shona. I had forgotten about Shona until last night."

"But nothing is going to happen to us at Shona."

"Oh! Isn't it? How do you know? If there's any-where on this river that the Germans will be watch-ing, it's Shona. That's where the road from the south crosses the river. Before the war, boats used to carry the Africans across there. The Germans will have people watching there. You can see right across the river there, and Shona is on a hill. The river is only half a mile wide; and they'll have guns."

"Then let's go past at night."

"That won't do, because the rapids start just below Shona. We can't go down those rapids in the dark. I'm not going down any rapids at all. We oughtn't to have come as far as this. It's all mad, silly. They might find us if they come out in a boat from Shona. I'm going back tomorrow – to that place we were in yesterday. That's the safest place for us."

He drank some more gin to show that he meant what he said.

Rose was white with anger, but she talked to Allnutt quietly and tried to make him change. It was useless. He sat silent and made no attempt to answer.

Rose sat in the stern of the launch while Allnutt

went on drinking. She was alone in a small boat with a drunken man! She sat there in the darkness, ready to fight for her life or against any attack on her. Every one of Allnutt's movements made her stand ready. There was a terrible time when Allnutt was reaching under the seat to find another bottle and she thought that he was coming towards her.

But Allnutt had no idea of attacking Rose. He thought of his mother, of his friends in London when he was a boy, and began to weep. Then he began to sing. And then he became sleepy. . . . He was asleep; Rose could hear him. Then there was a noise and Rose jumped up again, ready; but Allnutt had fallen on the floor with his cups and bottles. The smell of gin filled the air.

Allnutt went on sleeping.

Rose did not sleep. Her anger and her hatred of Allnutt kept her awake. She felt that she had no hope left. She knew that she could not put Allnutt on the land and go on by herself; but she wanted to go on: she wanted that more than anything on earth. There was nothing left to live for if she could not get the 'African Queen' down to the Lake to strike a blow for England. She hated Allnutt! As the night went on she decided to make him pay for this! She would make him sorry he had ever been born!

Towards morning Rose slept; but sleep did not make her cold anger and hatred any less.

Daylight showed Allnutt lying on the floor. His face was grey, and unpleasing sounds came from his mouth.

Rose stepped over him. She pulled out the case of

gin, took out a bottle and opened it. She poured the gin over the side and dropped the bottle after it.

When for the third time Allnutt heard the *glug-glug-glug* of poured liquid he opened his eyes and tried to sit up.

"Coo!" he said. His head felt red-hot and he could not raise it. His eyes could not bear the light.

Rose paid no attention to his cries of pain. She poured the last bottle from that case. She went forward and pulled out a second case from among the boxes and stores. She broke it open. Allnutt rolled over and looked at her. With great difficulty he sat up. He looked at her, not understanding what she was doing.

"Coo!" he said.

Rose wasted no time or pity on him. She went on pouring gin over the side. He got up on his knees; then with his body hanging over the side he drank the brown river-water. Rose felt that he might fall in; but she didn't care. Then he sat back and was sick, bringing up all the water which he had drunk.

Rose dropped the last bottle into the river. Then she went back to the stern, passing close enough to touch him, but she took no notice of him. She went up to the bow of the launch and washed herself; then she prepared her breakfast and ate it. She cleared it away, then came back to the stern, but still she gave him neither a look nor a word. She took out her dirty clothes and washed them over the side, then hung them up to dry!

Then she sat down and did nothing. She did not even look at Allnutt.

This was the beginning of the Great Silence.

She went on pouring gin over the side

During the morning Allnutt did not notice, but later on he became restless. He felt that by now he ought to be forgiven for his drinking, and he wanted to talk as much as he usually did: he found this Silence difficult to bear.

"Coo!" he said. "Isn't it hot?"

Rose paid him no attention.

"We could do with another storm. It does make you cool for a minute."

No answer. Rose got out her needle and began to repair her clothes. Needlework is a great help to a woman in a battle with a man. She is looking down at her work so that he cannot see her face, and she seems to be attending only to her work – not to him.

"Aren't you going to answer me, Miss? . . . I'm sorry for what I did last night . . . You've paid me back now, haven't you – pouring away the rest of the gin."

No answer.

"All right! Have it your own way, you . . . !" he said angrily. He moved restlessly about the boat. Then he cleaned and oiled the engine. Then he washed himself, put engine-oil on his hair and brushed it. He put everything away and sat down.

Five minutes later he was on his feet again moving about and wondering what he could do now. And the silence of the river was all around him.

Silence! Silence! It was driving him mad.

Five

SHONA

Allnutt made several attempts to make Rose talk, but he only once succeeded in making her say anything.

"I hate you," she said. "You are afraid and you tell lies, and I won't speak to you ever!"

At first Rose did not speak to Allnutt because she was angry: then she began to see that the Silence might make him obey. Her one fear was that Allnutt might attack her, but she was a big, strong woman, and she took the little knife out of her work-bag and put it ready for use if necessary.

Allnutt had no idea of attacking her. If there had been any gin left, he might have done so; but all the gin was in the river. He did not understand what he had done wrong. At first he thought it was because he got drunk. Her plan for going down the river was so mad that he hardly thought about it. At last he understood that Rose really meant to do it, and that she would not speak to him nor look at him till he agreed. So he continued to suffer for another twenty-four hours of silence.

Silence was one of the things which Allnutt could not bear. As a child he had lived in noisy streets, and later in among noisy machines and in noisy engine-rooms. He might have borne the silence of

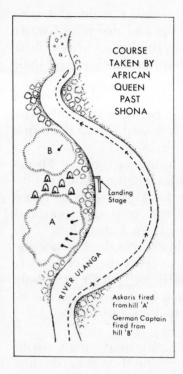

COURSE TAKEN BY AFRICAN QUEEN PAST SHONA

B

Landing Stage

A

RIVER ULANGA

Askaris fired from hill 'A'

German Captain fired from hill 'B'

The River at Shona

the river, but Rose's silent presence made it worse. That hurt his pride.

He could not sleep. Sleeplessness was quite a new thing to Allnutt: it troubled him very much. He lay awake for one whole night. He rolled about on his uncomfortable bed on the boxes of explosives. He sat up and smoked cigarettes. He tried again to sleep. He really thought that there was something seriously wrong with him.

In the morning, faced with another day of this, Allnutt gave in. "Let's hear what you want to do, Miss. Tell me and we'll do it."

"I want to go down the river," said Rose.

Once more Allnutt could see death in the rapids, or death wandering in the forest; or they might be taken prisoners by the Germans. He was afraid, and yet he felt that he could not stay another minute in this place. He must get away from it!

"All right, Miss," he said. "Come on."

The 'African Queen' went out of the side-stream

into the wide river. There was a wind and long waves moved the launch up and down and water came over the bows, *ss–ss–ss*, on the hot boiler. Rose sat at the tiller: she was happy: they were on their way again to help England.

"That's the hill where Shona stands," shouted Allnutt. Shona was a village between two hills. The river *bent* round the hills: it flowed round them in a great *bend,*– almost a half circle.

As the 'African Queen' came in sight of Shona Allnutt began to work on the engine to make it do its best. He would rather be killed than be taken prisoner. He hid behind the heap of wood and hoped it would stop a shot from hitting him.

The Askaris (African soldiers) on the hill saw the launch coming: they ran to fetch the German officer. Yes: that was the 'African Queen', the only launch on that river. He had been given special orders from von Hanneken to look out for her.

"Those missionaries and that man from Limbasi are tired of hiding," he thought, "or they have no more food and they are coming to give themselves up as prisoners. Yes, that's what they mean to do. There's no doubt about it. They're keeping to the far side of the river: they must be meaning to come to land below Shona, on the soft low land just round the hill, because just beyond Shona the river goes over the rapids, and no one can take a ship there."

He walked to the other side of the hill. The fools were still keeping to the further side: they showed no signs of coming in.

"God knows what they mean to do! But they must be stopped." He shouted and his twelve Askari soldiers came running to him.

"Get ready to fire! . . . . ."

They loaded. Some of them lay down to take aim: some remained standing.

"Fire!"

The launch kept on. "The fools must have heard the shots," he thought, "and some of the shots must have gone somewhere near."

"Again!" More shots: still no change of course on the launch. He seized a gun and lay down. He loaded and took aim. The sun was in his eyes: it was very easy to lose sight of the white awning of the boat and the distance was really too great.

He fired, loaded; fired again and again. The launch still kept on. Then trees came between him and the launch. He jumped up and ran along with his Askaris following. He ran across the village and up the path through the forest on the other side. When he reached the top he could look down on the last part of the river before the rapids. The launch was going towards them. He fired twice, though there was no chance of hitting them. Then they had gone round the corner out of sight.

"Von Hanneken will be very angry when he hears of the loss of the launch. But what more could I have done? No one could have expected this: no one but a madman would take a launch into those rapids. They are probably dead by now, broken to pieces among those rocks."

As the officer walked back to Shona he was still

undecided whether to report this to von Hanneken.
"Von Hanneken will be certain that it is my fault.
It would be better to say nothing about it. The
launch has gone and the poor devils in it are dead –
that foolish missionary and his ugly sister, and that
Englishman who worked in the mines. He had a
face like a rat. The world will not feel the loss of
them."

But he felt sorry for them —— poor devils!

Six

THE RAPIDS

Shona stood on a hill and the river flowed
round it in a great bend. Rose steered the 'African
Queen' round the outside of the bend. The river
was flowing faster than before as it came nearer to
the rapids, and it flowed fastest round the outside
of the bend.

Suddenly Rose heard the noise of shots.

"They've got us!" said Allnutt jumping up in the
middle of the boat. Rose paid no attention to him:
she was keeping the 'African Queen' in the fastest
water along the edge of the bank.

More shots came, but did not hit them. Rose
turned the tiller a little so as to get more in mid-
stream to take the second bend of the river. She was
attending so closely to her steering that she did
not hear the shot which came very close to her. A

moment later two shots hit the funnel. Allnutt turned with a jump. Rose pulled the tiller over and straightened the launch on her course. Then Shona disappeared behind the point of the hill. Allnutt stood up giving cries of victory and laughing at the enemy.

"The engine!" shouted Rose. "Look to it!"

They were flying along now, faster and faster: the river was becoming narrower and narrower and the stream stronger with every yard. Here and there were those dangerous rough waters which are a sign of hidden rocks. Rose steered carefully away from them. There was another bend. She pulled the tiller across. She could not see forward: the awning was in the way. She jumped up holding the tiller with her right knee: then with her left hand she roughly pulled away the awning from its supports. Neither of them noticed the last two shots which the officer fired at them.

The 'African Queen' swung round the corner: she rolled as she met the rough water there. There were rocks with white water boiling round them. She pulled the tiller over and the rocks seemed to rush by. Lower down there seemed to be almost a wall of rocks across the river: then she saw a channel just wide enough and turned the boat into it. Beyond it there was a long green waterfall. Just as the stern of the 'African Queen' rose up to go down it, Rose saw a black rock standing up right in her path at the bottom: it would take the bottom out of the ship if they touched it. She had to keep the boat straight on her course for a second, then

Rose fought with the tiller

she threw herself against the tiller to bring her over. For a moment it seemed as if the water would pull her against the rocks, but the engine forced the boat through the stream. They got through the narrow opening by inches. Rose fought with the tiller as they came into the wild waves at the tail of the rapid. Next moment they had reached the quiet of the deep water.

Allnutt had had no time to look about: he was far too busy keeping the engine running: he knew that their lives depended on it; but he felt the ship jump and roll beneath his feet and out of the corner of his eye he saw the rocks rush by at a speed which showed how great their own speed was. He prayed, "Our Father . . . . " He had not prayed since he left school.

After a few seconds they reached the next rapid. It was like the last one, – ugly rocks and rushing water. Rose's hand had to be firm and her eye quick. The touch of those rocks meant death. She felt such excitement as she had never felt before. Her mind was working like a machine. She forced the 'African Queen' to obey her and find a safe course through the dangers all around her.

Lower down, the river passed through a narrow channel with high walls of rock on each side. It was like riding in a very fast car. Then it turned the corner so quickly that it looked as if it flowed into the face of the rock. Rose kept close to the rock so that the 'African Queen' was beginning to turn just before she reached the bend. It was a good thing that she did this! The boat was carried by the force of the water over to the other bank: Rose pulled at the tiller with all her strength: the bow came round, but it seemed for a moment that the stern would be thrown against the rocks. The propeller battled with the stream and just saved them. Then the boat was thrown into mid-stream and Rose had to find a new course through rocks with white water boiling round them.

Later, she saw Allnutt trying to catch her attention. The noise of the waters was so great that he could not make his voice reach her. He stood up holding a piece of wood and waved a hand towards the shore. He was telling her that they needed more wood for the fire. She showed that she understood; then she had to look forward at the rocks. They passed through another set of rapids, then went through a narrow place only fifty yards wide where they seemed to be travelling with the speed of a train. They must find somewhere to stop soon, but there was nowhere in that narrow place where they could stop.

Allnutt was standing up again with his piece of wood. Rose waved him aside: she understood their need and their danger as well as he did. They went on.

Then Rose saw what she wanted. A wall of rocks ran almost across the stream, broken only in the centre where the water was heaped up and broke through in one great green wave. Below it there was clear water, and no rocks.

The bow of the 'African Queen' rose up as she hit the heaped-up water; then the stern came up and she shot down it. At the foot there were high green waves. The launch hit them with a *crash*. Water came over into the boat. It seemed as if the 'African Queen' would push her nose deeper and deeper while the water pushed against her raised-up stern. But at the last moment she freed herself. The launch came round. Rose threw her weight against the tiller. "Stop!" she shouted. The launch went slowly forward into a little piece of quiet water just below the wall of rocks. Close under her stern the river boiled over the rocks. Above them it beat against the wall of rocks which Rose had just escaped. There was noise all about them; but they were at peace.

"Coo!" said Allnutt, but he could not hear the word as he said it.

Rose felt herself weak in the knees, and she had a strange empty feeling inside. Both felt wildly excited by their success. Allnutt kept talking to Rose continuously although she could not hear a word he said.

This deep narrow place in the river was cool and pleasant. Above them trees grew to the edge of the cliffs so that the light which came through them was green and restful. For a time they were out of the heat and burning sunlight of Africa. There were no insects. There was no fear of discovery by the Germans.

Work on the boat had to be begun at once. Rose set up that devilish old pump and began to free the boat of the water which had come in. Allnutt went to get wood. The shore was covered with dry wood which had been brought down from above and caught up here. He brought loads of it to the launch.

They ate a big meal and drank many cups of tea with a lot of sugar in them. They could not talk because of the unending noise of the water, but they smiled at each other and made signs.

When they had eaten they began to feel sleepy. Rose felt herself going to sleep while Allnutt was putting the cups and plates away. Soon she was asleep. Allnutt lay down on the boxes of explosives. It was strange that the Great Silence had been only a day ago: it seemed like a memory of when he was a child. "Those Germans didn't believe that anyone could go down those rapids," he thought. "Well, we've shown them!"

He smiled and fell asleep.

Seven

THE BAY OF THE WATERFALL

Next morning Allnutt got up steam in the boiler and they heaped the boat with wood. Rose took her place at the tiller and looked down at the next rapid. She made signs to Allnutt: he pushed the boat out from the side. Then she made another sign, and he made the propeller turn backwards to get the bow clear of the bank. Then she made a sign to go forward. The launch went into the main stream and the madness of the day had begun.

Rose felt a wild joy in steering the launch into the waves, to feel her jump about under her and to see water come flying back over the bow. The finest feeling of all was the upward rise of the stern as the 'African Queen' reached the top of one of those long deep descents of green water and went racing down it with death on each side and destruction seeming to be waiting for them below.

Towards afternoon there were no more rapids. The river became wider, but the rocks on each side were like walls, and the river raced between them.

At last they found a place where they could anchor. A side-stream came into the river here. It came in a waterfall, forty feet high. Rose had just time to notice it and steer clear. Then she saw a wide place just below; the water had eaten away the bank there, making a little bay. She made a sign to Allnutt. The 'African Queen' came gently to a stop under the steep bank.

Allnutt tied up the launch to the shore while Rose looked about her.

"How beautiful!" she said. The bank was not so steep here. The face of the rock was covered with flowers. The rocks were red and brown and grey where they could be seen through the flowers. There was no dust: there were no flies. It was no hotter than a summer day in England. For once in her joyless life she felt pleased with herself: her body was full of life.

Allnutt came climbing back into the boat.

"Would you please look at my foot, Miss?" he

said. "I got a sharp bit of wood in it, and I think
it's still there."

Rose got down to her knees and took the shoe
off. She found the place and pulled out the bit of
wood and watched the blood come back again.

"There's nothing there now," she said, and let
his foot go.

"Thank you, Miss," said Allnutt.

He waited then, looking up at the flowers.

"Coo! it's pretty!"

The last twenty-four hours spent in the noise and
danger of the rapids made them feel closer com-
panions, and very happy.

"That waterfall there," said Allnutt, "makes me
think of ———"

He never said what it made him think. He looked
at Rose beside him.

He did not know what he was doing when he put
out his hand to her neck, sunburned and cool. Rose
caught at his hands to hold them, not to put them
away.

Eight

BROKEN PROPELLER

It was Rose who got up and prepared the
breakfast. It seemed wrong to her that Charlie (as
she now called him) should be troubled with such
woman's work; but he helped her.

Then Allnutt gathered wood and got up steam as usual.

"I think," he said, "that we have left the last rapid behind and this part of the river leads to the flat land round the Lake."

But he was wrong. After ten minutes of quiet water the noise of a rapid reached Rose's ears. She sat up, held the tiller firmly and looked forward to find a line of clear water through the rocks with no turn in it too sharp and sudden for the launch. This had to be done in the few seconds of time between seeing the rapid and the moment when the 'African Queen' began to be thrown about by the first waves.

So they went down the wild river. They passed each danger: it was surprising that they did it; but it was too much to hope that this would always be so. They came to a place where the channel was too narrow to offer a single inch of clear water. Rose had to choose a point where the water seemed a little quieter and try to judge from the parts of the rocks which she could see what course was taken by the water which boiled between them.

The bow of the 'African Queen' rose up, then fell into the meeting waves. She shook, and water flew back high over the top of the funnel. Rose saw clear water in front. Then, as the launch went through, there was a *crash* beneath her, followed by a shaking as if the boat would be shaken to pieces.

Allnutt shut off steam.

"Keep her going, Charlie," shouted Rose.

Allnutt opened the steam a little: the shaking began again, but the propeller was still turning and

Rose could still steer the 'African Queen'. Allnutt prayed that the bottom would not come out of the boat. Rose looked over the side; she could see that they were going forward slowly through the water while the river hurried them on at its usual speed.

Rose understood that it was very important that they should stop as soon as possible; but where could she stop in that narrow channel with the water rushing through? With that small speed she would never be able to steer the 'African Queen' down a rapid. She moved the tiller and found that there was something seriously wrong with the steering. The propeller seemed to turn the boat sideways and it needed a lot of tiller to correct this.

The cliffs rushed by on either side and the shaking seemed to get worse. She fought to keep the boat in mid-stream. A long way in front she could see dark rocks standing up out of the river with white water around them. She must stop! Down on the left there was a big rock: it stood out from the side into the river. It might be possible to stop and be safe below it.

"Charlie!" she shouted. He heard and understood the signs which she made. It would be difficult. If they turned too soon they would be thrown against the rock: if they turned too late they would be carried stern first and helpless down the rapid. Rose had to allow for the changed speed of the boat, and for this new sideways drive of the propeller.

She put the tiller across and watched the bow as the boat came round. The bow came up behind the rock, but the turn was not complete. The launch still lay partly across the river. The bow was touching the bottom. The launch rolled over: a mass of water came in over the side: it put out the boiler-fire.

Allnutt saved the ship. He jumped over the side into the water. He got his shoulder under the bow and pushed. The bow came off the ground where she was stuck and the pull of the stream began to take the launch down the stream, but Allnutt had the rope from the bow. He put it round a point of rock and held it. The boat moved slowly in towards the shore. Five seconds later she was in the quiet water below the rock, while Allnutt fixed several ropes to hold her to the land.

The 'African Queen' was nearly full of water. Rose stood up on the highest place in the stern, but the water was round her feet. She was just able to smile at Charlie. She was feeling sick and faint. The thought of that green wave coming over the side still troubled her. Allnutt sat down on a rock and smiled back at her.

"We were nearly finished that time," he said. She could not hear what he said but clearly he was quite calm. Rose sat on the side of the boat and kept her feet out of the water. She would not let her weakness be seen.

Allnutt came up into the boat. He looked round. "Coo!" he said. "What a state she's in! I wonder how much stores we've lost."

"Let's get this water out and see," said Rose.

They both worked hard throwing out the water over the side: soon Rose was getting out the pump so as to pump out the water which remained below the floor.

"Here! I'll do that, Rosie," said Allnutt.

"No. Sit down and rest yourself – And don't catch cold."

Rose felt that pumping out the boat was like cleaning a room – a woman's work.

"The first question is," said Allnutt as the pumping was finished, "how much water is coming in?" He took up some of the floor-boards. After half an hour there was no increase in the water.

"Coo!" said Allnutt. "That's better than we could have hoped for. I would have expected to find a hole after all that. And we haven't lost any stores."

"What was that noise and shaking just before we stopped?"

"I've still got to find out," said Allnutt.

He feared the worst, but he knew how sorry Rose would be if it was as bad as he feared.

"How are you going to do that?" asked Rose.

"I'll have to go down under the boat and look. You must stand there with that rope. There may be a stream under the boat which might carry me away."

Rose looked down and saw Allnutt disappear under the bottom of the boat. His feet could still be seen.

Then Allnutt came out and stood on the bottom beside the boat. The water ran down from his hair.

"Did you see anything, dear?" asked Rose.

"Yes," said Allnutt. He said no more till he had climbed back into the boat. He wanted time to think. Rose sat beside him and waited. She put out her dry hand and held his wet one.

"The propeller *shaft*[1] is badly bent, and one *blade*[1] has gone off the propeller."

[1]See picture of 'African Queen' on page 7.

"We'll have to repair it," said Rose. She had no idea of the seriousness of the thing.

"Repair it!" said Allnutt. He laughed. Already he could see himself and Rose wandering through the forest sick and hungry.

"God only knows how the shaft held on while we were getting in here."

"All right," said Rose. "Let's get everything dry, and have some dinner; and then we can talk about it."

Later, with some food in him and strong tea, Allnutt felt better.

"What shall we have to do before we go on?" she asked.

"I'll tell you what we could do if we had a place where we could pull the launch up out of the water, and if we had a machine shop, and if there was a port here to bring us the new parts we need. We would pull the ship up, take out the shaft and straighten it and write to the makers and get a new propeller. While we were waiting we could paint the bottom. Then we could put in the shaft and the new propeller and put her back in the water and go on as if nothing had happened. . . . But we haven't got anything. We've got nothing. And so we can't."

Allnutt was still thinking about wandering in the forest; but Rose could not imagine a man finding anything impossible.

"Can't we get the shaft off without pulling up the boat onto the shore?" she asked.

"I might," said Allnutt. "It means going under

water and getting the propeller off. I could do it, perhaps."

"Well, if you had the shaft up on the shore you could straighten it."

"No hope of that!" said Allnutt. "I would have to heat it, and have a flat thing to beat it on. But we've got no coal – nothing. And I don't know that sort of work."

"I saw an African – a Masai – working on iron. He had a wood fire and he beat the metal on a big stone. He had a boy to blow up the fire and make it hotter."

"We might try it," said Allnutt. "There's plenty of wood washed up by the river on the bank."

"Well, then ——" said Rose.

It was not easy to make Allnutt agree. He was an engineer – a man trained to do exact work with engines: he did not believe in rough inexact work. But, pressed by Rose, he was just beginning to decide to try to repair the shaft. Then suddenly he turned away from the idea again.

"No!" he said. "It's no use. I was forgetting the propeller. It's no use with one blade gone."

"It got us along a little," said Rose.

"If we used it with only two blades it would bend the shaft again," said Allnutt.

"Well, you'll have to make another blade. There's lots of metal which you could use."

"And tie it on, I suppose?" said Allnutt.

But Rose did not laugh as Allnutt expected. She took the idea seriously.

"Yes", she said, "if you think that will do. But

couldn't you stick it on somehow? Hammer the
two edges together when they are both very hot.
Weld it. That's the right word for hammering pieces
of hot metal together to join them, isn't it? Weld
it on."

"Coo!" said Allnutt. "You are funny! Really you
are!"

Allnutt imagined himself making a propeller
blade out of bits of metal, welding it by hand onto
the propeller and fixing this propeller onto a shaft
roughly straightened by hammering it on a rock,
and then expecting the 'African Queen' to go! He
laughed at the idea. He laughed and laughed, and
Rose had to laugh with him because by now they
loved each other so much.

After a time Rose said, "Why did you laugh like
that when I spoke of welding? Wasn't it the right
word?"

"Coo!" said Allnutt. "Well, listen and I'll ex-
plain. . . ."

But it was impossible to refuse Rose. In the end
Allnutt said, "Well, I'll see what I can do" – just
like any loving husband when asked to buy a lot of
new furniture. So they set to work.

After much work under the water, Allnutt succeeded in getting the propeller off and out of the
water. The missing blade had not broken away completely. There were about two inches of it remaining;
so it seemed more possible to fix on a new blade.

Allnutt next set himself to getting the shaft free: if
he could not repair that, it was useless to work on
the propeller.

Freeing the shaft was a very long and difficult task. It needed one person working inside the boat and one under the boat, and Rose had to learn a set of signs which Allnutt gave from below.

Before he had finished, Allnutt was able to hold his breath for a surprisingly long time; but, as a result of staying so long in the water and coming out into the hot sun his skin came off in thin pieces all over him. It was a wonderful moment for Rose when she saw the shaft move out, and Allnutt came up beside the boat with it in his hands.

Allnutt shook his head sadly over the bends now seen clearly in the light of day, but the two set themselves bravely to the task of making it straight again.

Allnutt made a *bellows,* – something which blows air – out of two pieces of flat wood and some leather from a coat which Rose had carried in her box for ten years of African life without wearing it. They found a good place for the fire. Allnutt found that, if Rose worked hard at the bellows, they could get the shaft hot enough for him to change its shape with his hammer.

Rose knelt beside the fire working the bellows like a mad woman! Her face was burnt. The fire used up wood so fast that soon Allnutt had gathered every bit of wood on the shore, and both had to climb up into the forest and pull wood to the top of the cliff and push it over the edge. Some of it was caught up on the cliff or fell into the river. But they got enough.

But they were as happy as children during all this hard work. Hard labour suited both of them.

Allnutt was filled with Rose's eagerness to complete the work, and every evening there was that wonderful feeling of friendliness which drew them closer together. Rose had never known such happiness before; nor, perhaps, had Allnutt.

Little by little the propeller shaft was straightened. At last the morning came when Allnutt was satisfied and he was able to say that the shaft was as good as he could make it. He could now turn to the much more difficult task of the propeller.

He found a suitable piece of metal and beat it and shaped it until it began to look like the other two blades. Rose took care of the fire, and worked the bellows. She held the end of the piece of metal: it was supposed to be cool, but she held it in a cloth, and she burnt her fingers again and again, and her nose was filled with the smell of burning cloth. Nearly every piece of clothing which she and Allnutt possessed had holes burnt in it. But she enjoyed every minute of it.

"If my father," said Allnutt once, "had put me to this sort of work when I was a boy, I don't think I would ever have come to Africa. Coo! I might still be. . . ."

Allnutt thought of a London working-class shopping street on a Saturday night – the smell of the fish-shop, the bright lights, the crowds of people. For a moment he felt a wish to be back there; then he came back to real life again, the red cliffs, the singing river and the 'African Queen' down below, and Rose beside him.

"But then I should never have met you, Rose." He fingered the unfinished propeller blade. "Nor have done all this. It's worth it. It really is! I mean it."

Later the propeller blade began to need exact measurements and Allnutt had to make instruments which would make sure that it was exactly the same shape as the other two. Then he had to make a piece which would fit round part of the new blade and round the broken end of the old blade. Then he had to fix this in place.

At last the new blade was in place: it looked exactly like the others.

"There! That ought to do now," said Allnutt. "Let's hope it does."

Putting the shaft back in place and fixing the propeller onto it needed some more work below the water. When they were in place Allnutt got up steam in the boiler and sent the launch forward a little till it pulled hard on the rope holding it to the bank; then back to pull on the other ropes. This showed that the shaft and propeller would turn, but it did not prove that it would stand up to real work. They would find that in the rapids, with death as the answer if Allnutt's work failed.

They knew their danger but neither spoke of it. In the morning, still nothing was said. Allnutt got up steam in the boiler; there was plenty of wood; they were quite ready to go. Allnutt looked about him for the last time – at the rock-built fireplace, the heap of burnt wood. He turned to Rose standing beside the tiller: she could not speak but could only answer with a little movement of her head. He threw off the ropes from the bank, and pushed the

'African Queen' out from the bank. Then he turned the steam into the engine.

"Goodbye, dear," said Allnutt as he bent over the engine.

"Goodbye, dear," said Rose at the tiller.

Neither of them heard the other because of the noise of the river and the steam; neither was meant to hear, but there was high courage in them both.

The 'African Queen' went out into the stream. For a moment both felt as if something was wrong because the shaft did not make the same noise as it had done before: it was straighter than it had been before the accident. Rose put the tiller across and the launch turned towards the rapids. Next moment they were flying down stream with Allnutt watching the engine and Rose at the tiller looking forward to find her way through the rocks and rushing water which lay before her.

Nine

INSECTS

Below the last rapids there was a great change in the river. The bottom of the river was flat: the speed of the flow became less, and the character of the banks changed also.

A great deal of mud had been carried down by the river running at high speed over the rapids; here it fell to the bottom: the river spread out and formed

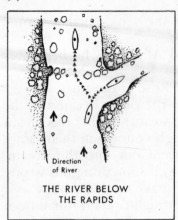

**THE RIVER BELOW
THE RAPIDS**

Direction
of River

many islands. Lower
down it spread out still
more into low wet land,
half mud and half water
steaming in the heat
and overgrown with a
thick covering of tall
grasses and other plants
and trees.

Rose and Allnutt soon
noticed the change. For
some time the river flow-
ed as fast as before and
Rose had to plan a course half a mile in front of
her, choosing some deep channel. She had to
choose a channel which would not end suddenly. If
she made a mistake the ship would be hurried along
until it hit the bottom; the propeller would be
broken again and the shaft bent, and the boat
would be buried by water heaping up against the
sides. Rose would not let herself think of these dangers but gave all her attention to seeing that the
channels which she chose did not come to that sort
of end.

The weather changed suddenly. Great black
clouds came rushing up into the sky. Then the
storm began and rain poured down. At the first
sight of the storm Rose began to steer the 'African
Queen' towards the shore. Allnutt tied the boat to
a tree growing on the edge of the water. There they
sat uncomfortably through the storm. The rain beat
down upon them. There was no awning now to
protect them. A warm wind came and Allnutt had

to hold the boat out from the shore for fear that the wind might blow her onto the land and endanger the shaft and propeller.

At last the storm passed, as quickly as it had come. The afternoon sun came out: the water steamed. The boat was half filled with water and they had to pump it out.

When the rain ended, the flies and other insects came, clouds of them hungry for blood. They were ten – twenty times as bad as those which they had known on the upper part of the river. Here there was a new sort of fly, a small black one, which bit like a red-hot needle and left a drop of blood at every bite. They flew into their eyes and noses and mouths, biting every piece of skin they could get at.

Their attacks did not become less in the evening or at night. It seemed impossible to hope for sleep in this steamy heat and under the unending attacks of these enemies: yet they were both worn out with the excitement of the day.

Some time in the night Allnutt came to Rose: "Here, try this: it can't be any worse." He had found the old awning which Rose had pulled down. It seemed as if they might die of heat under any sort of covering. They pulled the awning over their faces and ears. The heat was easier to bear than the insects. They slept at last, half boiled and hardly able to breathe. They awoke in the morning with very painful heads and dry mouths. And the insects still attacked them.

They had to make their way through evil-

smelling mud to find wood. Although every movement was painful they had to make six journeys.
But, once the ship was moving they were freed from
the insects.

The water was now brown, and its speed was less.
The river was half a mile wide. On each bank there
were very tall grasses and water-plants, and beyond
that the forest.

There was no need to keep watch for rapids and
rocks, but there was a lot of stuff in the water –
plants and branches and trees which might be a
danger to the propeller. Rose steered close to each
mass and she and Allnutt were able to pull in bits of
wood for use in the fire.

When evening came Allnutt said, "We need not
tie up to the bank tonight. The bottom is muddy:
we can use the anchor again. There won't be any
insects."

They put up what remained of the awning.

"Well," said Allnutt, "we've done it! We got
down the Ulanga. I didn't think it could be done.
It was you who said that it could. If it hadn't been
for you we shouldn't be here now. Don't you feel
proud of yourself?"

"No," said Rose. "Of course not. It was you who
did it. You made the engine go, and you repaired
the propeller . . . I don't think there's another
man alive who could have done it."

"I don't think anyone else will try," said Allnutt.

"We'll have a good supper tonight," said Rose,
jumping up. "No, don't you move. You just sit and
smoke your cigarette."

They had a good supper of all the nicest things

which the headman at the mine got for his dinner –
tinned fish and tinned beans and tinned fruit and
tinned milk.

The night came down. The river spread out on
each side in the starlight. The water was like black
glass, and deep within it the stars shone like real
things. They felt as if they were hanging high above
the earth with skies above and below.

Ten

REEDS

They went on down the wide black river: the
water was like glass as they came to it, and behind
them they left a V-shaped wave spreading further
and further as far as the eye could see until it
reached the bank covered with tall grasses and
even taller *reeds*.[1]

They went on, following the wide bends of the
river. They were hardly able to breathe in the heat.
The steam rising from the water made the distance
faint and unreal.

Rose brought the 'African Queen' slowly round
one more bend. She could not see the future course
of the river. Should she turn to the left or to the
right at this bend? It did not matter here, where the
river was so wide and so deep. She went on down
the middle of the channel, about a quarter of a mile

[1] *Reed* = tall water-plant.

from each shore, hoping to see the direction of the
next bend when it came nearer.

Then, slowly, she knew that the river had become
wider. They were further from both banks now. She
kept the 'African Queen' on the same course towards the forest far away and dimly seen in front of
her. She was sure that soon she would see the channel round the next bend.

After half an hour she still could not see the
channel. They were coming near the dark green
of the forest and the lighter green of the reeds. Rose
could see the whole length of it clearly: there was
no opening in it, no way through. The river must
have turned back upon itself. She moved the tiller
to go to the left bank again: it was the same here –
an unbroken line of reeds and the forest. It did not
seem as if the river flowed out in this direction.

"Perhaps the river ends here?" she thought.
"No! That's silly! Rivers don't end suddenly except
in sandy deserts. They don't end in rain forests like
this."

There was only one thing which she could do
which might help them. She steered the 'African
Queen' along the edge of the reeds.

"I am sure to find out what happens to the river if
I keep along its bank for long enough."

"What do you think this place is?" called Allnutt
from the bow.

"I don't know," said Rose. "I'll tell you soon."

They went on along the line of reeds. The water
seemed different: it was blacker, and moved very
slowly, and there were far more dead plants and

branches lying in the water. It seemed as if they had
reached the end of the river; – yet this was impossible.

"I don't know where we've come to," said Allnutt.
"But there's a lot of wood here. Let's stop and fill
up while we can."

Allnutt pulled the wood out of the water, cut it
into short lengths with his axe and spread it out to
dry. In the hot sun it would soon be dry enough to
burn.

"I think we've got enough now," he said at last.

They went on along the reeds. They seemed to be
going in a wide circle. Rose looked at the sun and
she could see that they were going in the opposite
direction from where they entered. On their left
the bank of reeds became wider and wider. It was
now so wide that they could hardly see the forest
beyond it.

"But the river must find a way out somewhere
along here," thought Rose. "It's half a mile wide;
it must have a way out. Soon we'll come to it."

Afternoon came and still they could see no
break. In some places there were signs of very small
channels through the reeds – places where the reeds
were not quite so thick, showing that there was
deeper water below them.

Now, judging by the sun, they were nearly on the
same course as they were when Rose first noticed
that the river had become wider. So they must have
come round in almost a full circle. After another
ten minutes Rose knew that this was so! They were
back again where they had started: they were going

towards the rapids.

A week ago she would have wept with shame; but she was different now. There was hardly anything which an African river could do which would surprise her. But, if she was a fool, so was Allnutt. When she told him to stop, he was surprised. He looked about him but he did not understand where he was. He thought that Rose had found the way out to the Lake.

"Drop the anchor," she said. "Now, do you see that the river is flowing in the opposite direction – towards the rapids, away from the Lake?"

"Well, these banks look all the same to me. . . . But here we are and we've got a good place for the night. No insects. We may as well be comfortable and forget about things."

"All right," said Rose, but she still stood shading her eyes and looking across the water to the opposite shore. "There must be a way out," she said. "I noticed a lot of little channels through the reeds but would not take them. We'll choose the best one tomorrow and get through somehow. We can't be very far from the Lake."

Rose did not have a peaceful night. She was angry because they had got no further forward in that day.

She was not used to failure and was angry with herself. She lay awake for a long time and was angry at Allnutt's peaceful sleeping. Next morning she said few words and spoke sharply. Allnutt looked at her when she gave a short answer to his usual flow of talk. He decided to say no more, but shook his head and felt very wise as he thought over the mysterious ways of women. He made ready to start as quickly as possible.

Rose steered the 'African Queen' straight across towards the place where she would find the best channel through the reeds.

"Go slower now," she called.

They went as close to the edge of the reeds as they dared. She saw two places where the reeds did not grow so thickly, but each time, after a moment's doubt, she went on past them. Then they reached a broader, clearer passage. She turned the boat into the opening.

Allnutt turned off the engine till the propeller was hardly turning. He did not want to have any trouble with that propeller. He felt the bottom with the boat-hook. It seemed that reeds could not grow where the water was deep enough for the 'African Queen' to pass.

Now the channel divided into two and Rose had to choose. Rose turned the boat into what seemed to be the better one. As they went on, the reeds became thicker and thicker. Then the 'African Queen' stopped. Allnutt quickly shut off the steam.

"We've run onto the ground," he said.

"I know," said Rose; "but we've got to go on. We must pull her along by the reeds. The launch will go through mud like this, but we can't use the propeller."

So they went on. Allnutt in the bow reached forward with the boat-hook then pulled the boat forward two feet. Rose pulled at the reeds which she could reach over the side.

It was hot. The reeds shut off any wind: the sun
shone down on them. Soon the insects found them
and came in clouds. The work was very hard. After
two hours Allnutt was breathing heavily and when
he opened his mouth to draw in the air, the insects
were drawn in with it.

"I'm sorry," he said at last. "I can't keep on at
this!"

"All right," said Rose. "Give me the boat-hook."

"The work's very heavy," said Allnutt. Rose took
no notice, but climbed past him into the bow with
the boat-hook in her hand. Allnutt fell into the
bottom of the boat. For Rose he had worked till he
dropped.

Rose found the work heavy. It needed all the
strength she had. It did not take long to tire her
out. At last she put down the boat-hook and lay
down in the stern of the boat. The flies followed
her in thousands.

"We'll go on again tomorrow," she said.

The reeds were now higher and they were in the
shade, but the boat was almost too hot to touch.
The flies were worse than ever. After some time
Rose stood up and tried to see where they were.
She had not expected to take a whole day in getting
through the reeds, but the first day was ended and
they were only half way in. There was nothing to
show that they would ever get through at all.

Anyone less brave than Rose might have begun to
wonder what would happen to them if they found it
impossible to go on. There was no chance of pulling
the launch, stern first, back the way they had come.
They would be held in this place until their food

came to an end and they died, – or until they were
drowned in the mud trying to reach the shore on
foot. But Rose did not try to imagine what might
be. "If we fail, it would not be because we have not
tried hard enough": that is what Rose was saying to
herself as she fought the flies.

Eleven

STILL TRYING

There was no need to tie up the boat that night:
it seemed as if nothing could move them. They
hardly felt the wind which came with the storm
during that night. It bent the reeds over the boat,
but sitting under this roof of reeds they did not
notice the wind. They sat there suffering the rain
as it poured down on them.

"There's one thing about this," said Allnutt. "It
may make the water deeper. Even half an inch would
make a big difference. It can't rain too much for
me."

Later that night, long after the rain had stopped,
Rose suddenly heard a noise. Allnutt had gone to
sleep. It was only the smallest possible sound, a
faint whispering. It was the noise of running water.
This gentle sound came from all around, – water
brought down by the river was finding its way
through the reeds.

Before Allnutt woke up, Rose was standing there trying to decide what course to take. Then Allnutt came up into the bow of the boat to begin the day's labour.

"I think we are off the ground," he said. He took the boat-hook and reached forward. "Yes; there's no doubt about it. If there were not these reeds. . . ."

The channel was narrower here and the reeds caught against the sides as they moved along. Some were pressed down under the boat. Each pull seemed to bring the boat forward less: sometimes she went back a few inches. Rose was able to help by running about the boat freeing the sides from the reeds which were holding her back.

They moved on, slowly but hopefully. They could see by the sun that they were going in the general direction of the Lake.

Suddenly Allnutt gave a cry of joy: "There's another channel here." Rose climbed up quickly into the bow to see.

Yes: they had found another channel and the water was more free from reeds, and they could see that it was moving: it was very slow, but it was moving!

"Coo!" said Allnutt. "Look at that! Look out, Rose, there will be rapids next!"

They could still laugh.

It was delightful to feel the boat moving freely again. He put the boat-hook round a root and pulled hard. The boat went four feet through the water, and went on moving while Allnutt was finding another place for his boat-hook.

"Coo!" he said. "We're going several miles an hour!"

They came round a bend and Rose could see the trees on the bank straight in front. The channel became wider. There were no more reeds. The 'African Queen' moved forward slowly a little, then stopped. They were in a small lake with trees on the far side. It was covered with *water-lilies*. They had red and white flowers and they grew so closely together that the water could not be seen. There was a smell of decay. On the far bank there were trees, growing in strange shapes covered with climbing plants.

"It's not going to be easy getting her through that," said Allnutt.

"There's a channel over there," said Rose, pointing.

"I expect you are right," said Allnutt. "All we've got to do now is to get there!"

They had met a place like this higher up the river, – water covered with water-lilies. There it was small and they got out of it easily, but here they had to go through a hundred yards of it.

"Let's try it," said Rose.

"Of course we're going to try it," said Allnutt, rather hurt by her words. "Of course we are!"

It was not easy. There was nothing to take hold of to pull themselves along; but the plants pressed so close against the boat that they held her back as much as the reeds had done. Allnutt felt that the plants were being caught in the propeller. The bottom was mud – so soft that it was useless to push the boat-hook into it. When he pulled it out the boat moved back as far as it had moved forward, and evil-smelling gas came up through the water.

"Can't we try rowing?" said Rose.

"We might," said Allnutt.

They took flat pieces of wood and tried. It was very slow, and very difficult because they had to bend over the side in a very uncomfortable way, and after a few minutes there was unbearable pain under the arm. She and Allnutt kept on changing sides because of this.

They moved so slowly that they did not notice when they ceased to move at all. They went on working: then they looked round at each other.

"We are caught up on something," said Allnutt.

"Yes."

"It's that propeller... There's only one thing to do." He took out his knife.

Rose wanted to stop him: in that mass of plants it might be dangerous; but Allnutt must chance the danger or they could not go on.

"We'll have to be careful," she said. It was all that she could say.

"Yes," said Allnutt. "I'll tie this rope round me. You count fifty from the time I go under, and if I'm not coming up by then, pull the rope, and pull, and go on pulling."

"All right," said Rose.

He put his legs over the side. Those plants were not the only danger: there might be something worse, – much worse. Rose did not guess the sick fear which was in him. Holding his knife he dropped into the water. He breathed deeply several times: then his head went under and his legs disappeared. Rose began to count. At 'thirty' she began to pull the rope. . . . Allnutt came up. He had to pull the stuff away from his face before he could breathe or see.

"There's a great mass of it round the propeller. It is easy to cut it. I've done a lot already. Well, down I go again!"

After the fourth time Allnutt smiled: "All clear!" he said. "Hold the knife: I'm coming in."

Rose helped him to clear the masses of water-plants from his body. Then she gave a little cry.

On Allnutt's body and arms and legs there were *leeches* – little black creatures which fix themselves on the skin and draw out the blood. Allnutt felt sick at the sight of them.

"Can't you pull them off?" he said faintly.

"No. I mustn't do that: that would poison the wound. Salt gets them off." She ran to fetch the tin of salt. The leeches dropped on the floor. Allnutt put his foot on the first one and blood – his own blood – came out under his foot. Rose threw the rest of them in the river. Blood was still running down and drying on Allnutt's body under the hot sun. At last the blood stopped.

"Let's get away from here," he said. He hated leeches more than anything on earth.

They went on, – slowly, very slowly. Afternoon came and some of the red flowers began to close.

The sun was lower now. There was a line of shade at the edge, near the trees. The 'African Queen' reached it. The shade moved up to the stern of the boat, and Allnutt dropped his piece of wood.

"I can't do any more," he said, nearly weeping. He turned away from Rose so that she should not see.

When he had eaten and drunk, he felt better. Later in the evening he was able to laugh.

"We've come here by steam, and we've pulled the boat along with the boat-hook, and we've pushed her along with these bits of wood. What we haven't done yet is to get out and carry her. I suppose that will come next."

Rose remembered these words later on the following day. That did come next.

Twelve

MANGROVES

In the morning there was only a narrow line of water-lilies to cross. They fought their way across it with new hope. They could see the beginnings of a channel. Nothing could be worse than those water-lilies.

The trees were called *mangroves*. Where the mangroves began the water-lilies ended: they could not live in the deep shade of the mangroves.

They reached the mouth of the channel, and looked along it. The trees made a wall on each side and a roof over it. It was very dark, and the smell of decay filled their noses; but they were glad to find any place, however ugly, if the way through it was easy.

When they came out from the water-lilies they stopped and looked down into the water.

"Coo!" said Allnutt angrily. "It's grass now!"

The grass grew up from the bottom almost filling the water.

"We can't go by steam here," he said. "We would never get the propeller to turn in that stuff."

Rose looked: any other channel would be just as bad. "Come on!" she said. They went on pushing the boat forward with their pieces of wood. It was fearfully hot, they could hardly breathe, the water was half water and half mud.

"Shall I try with the boat-hook – hooking her along? We would get along better that way."

"We could both use hooks here," said Rose. "Can you make a hook?"

"Easy," said Allnutt. He beat a metal hook out of an iron bar and fixed it to a wooden shaft.

With both using hooks they got along faster. They stood side by side in the bow hooking onto branches or roots in front. They were travelling at about half a mile an hour. Rose thought, "If this mangrove forest is ten miles wide, we may be through it in twenty or thirty hours." But it took much longer than that.

They soon had to take down the funnel and the awning so as to go under branches hanging low over the water. There were roots which reached across the channel below the water. Sometimes feeling with the boat-hook they could find a deeper place where they got across, or got round. Sometimes Allnutt had to get out, make his way forward through the mud and pull the 'African Queen' over the roots. Rose remembered his words about "getting out and carrying the boat."

If there was no way over or round they both sat down in the mud and made cuts in the root to break it. Mud spread over everything, and with it came the smell. In the half-light they had to look at everything twice to make sure what it was: it might be a snake whose bite might be death.

The biting insects had given them an illness called *Malaria*: every morning they lay feeling icy cold and helpless, and then the cold passed and they felt burning hot. At last they slept for an hour or two and woke up able to move about and go on.

The channel bent this way and that way and they had no idea in what direction they were going. When another channel joined they had to look and see which way the water was flowing by dropping bits of wood in it.

They never saw the sun in that forest of darkness. Days came and went: it was day when there was enough light to see and night when it was too dark to do any more. They did not know how many days passed. They ate very little: the food smelled of mud and decay. It was a worse life than any animal's life. And all the time they were afraid for the propeller. There must never be a moment's carelessness or it might be broken again. The launch must be moved round a corner inch by inch because the propeller might come sideways against some hidden roots.

At last another large channel came in and they began to feel hope. The branches were thinner above them: the channel was deep and wide. Then the channel became so broad that sunlight reached them.

"Do you think we've got through, Rose?"

She hooked a root and gave a hard pull before answering.

"Yes," she said at last. "I think we have."

They smiled at each other across the boat. They were a fearful sight! They were covered with mud. Their hair was thick with mud. Their faces were white and their skins yellow from the malaria and their eyes were deep-set. They looked more like wild men from thousands of years ago than the sister of a missionary and a trained engineer. But they still smiled at each other.

The channel took another turn. There were no more mangrove trees.

"Reeds!" whispered Allnutt. "Reeds!" He had dealt with reeds before: they were better than mangroves.

Rose stood up in the bow and looked over the reeds as far as she could see.

"The Lake is just on the other side of the reeds," she said.

She immediately began to think of what must be done next. "How much wood have we got?" she asked.

"Quite a lot," said Allnutt. "About enough for half a day."

'We ought to have more than that."

Out on the Lake it would not be so easy to get wood. They must have plenty for the task which lay before them. "Let's stop and get some."

Allnutt did not like it, nor did she; but it had to be done. Now they had seen the blue sky, they were madly eager to get away from those hated mangroves without a moment's delay.

"Green wood is not much good under our boiler," said Allnutt.

"It's better than nothing," answered Rose. "And I expect it will have a day or two to dry off before we want it."

They looked at each other. All this journey had been made for one purpose–to torpedo the 'Louisa'! That purpose which had once seemed so mad to Allnutt was now near. But he had not thought about it for weeks. He knew that quite soon he would have to decide about it.

He tied up the 'African Queen' against the mangroves, took his axe and made a great heap of wood in the boat.

Now at last they could leave the mangroves for the happy safety of the reeds.

Thirteen

FIRST SIGHT OF THE ENEMY

There was a channel through the reeds. As soon as they turned one corner the Lake opened up in front of them – golden water as far as they could see with only one or two tree-covered islands. There were reeds on each side of the channel, but these did not matter: there was clear water forty miles broad and eighty miles long in front of them, with no rocks, no water-lilies, no mangroves. They felt free – wonderfully free! They felt like animals escaped from a cage. They slept more peacefully that night than they had done for many days.

Next morning they did not talk about torpedoing the 'Louisa'. Rose always liked to complete one step before thinking about the next.

"Let's get the boat cleaned," she said. "I can't bear this mud and smell."

The water round the launch was clear and clean. They washed out the whole boat. They took up the floor and cleaned out the evil-smelling water below. They washed all their clothes, and they washed themselves. It was wonderful to put on fresh clean clothes.

That night Rose thought of something which she had completely forgotten ever since she left the mission house. She had not said her prayers since she joined the 'African Queen': she had not even thought about God. Surely God would be angry with her! She quickly got down on her knees and bowed her head. Allnutt, waking in the night, saw her lift her face to heaven and saw her lips moving. He did not pray; he had forgotten how to pray. The fact that Rose was able to pray showed how much better she was than he. But he was content to leave to her the prayers for God's help in their dangers, just as he had left to her the steering through the rapids. He closed his eyes and went to sleep again.

Rose prayed that God would look with favour on the 'African Queen' and help them to find the 'Louisa' and torpedo her.

At last she lay down to sleep: she was quite calm again. She felt certain of the success of the blow which she would strike for England. Next morning when she awoke she prayed again for a moment on her knees while Allnutt stood uncomfortably in the bow, waiting. She was her old self again – with firm lips and a calm face as she looked out over the Lake.

There was something in sight there. It was not a cloud. It was black smoke, with a little white thing below it. She forced herself to speak quietly:

"Charlie," she said. "Come up here. What's that?"

One quick look was enough for Allnutt. "That's the 'Louisa'."

"Which way are they going?" asked Rose. Then, before he could answer, she said, "They're coming this way." She must be calm. "They must not see us. Can't we get back further among the reeds?"

"They'll see the funnel and awning," said Allnutt. They had put them back yesterday when they cleaned the boat.

Rose pulled down the awning again from its supports.

"You've got plenty of time to get the funnel down," she said. "They won't be able to see it yet and the reeds are between them and us."

If the 'Louisa' had been only a very small spot to them, they must be less than that to it.

With the funnel and the awning down they would be quite safe among the reeds, unless they were looked for specially; but the Germans would have no idea that the 'African Queen' was on the Lake.

She watched the 'Louisa' carefully: she was nearer now, moving south along the edge of the Lake. She was larger now, but it would be an hour before she came to the mouth of the river and might see the 'African Queen' against the reeds.

"Let's get the boat in now," she said.

They turned the launch so that the bow pointed into the reeds. Then they pulled with the boat-hooks and got her halfway in, but the stern was still outside.

"You must cut some of those reeds down. How deep is the mud?" said Rose.

Allnutt pushed the boat-hook down into the mud, and looked doubtfully at the result.

"Hurry up!" said Rose. He took his knife and went over the side. He went down in the mud till only his arms were above the water. Then he cut every reed he could reach; he cut them as low down as possible. Then he pulled himself up into the boat and Rose pulled the 'African Queen' into the space which he had made.

"There's a bit still outside," she said. "Once more will do it."

Allnutt went down among the reeds again and went on cutting. He climbed up again and they both pulled the boat into the cleared space. The reeds which had been pushed aside closed behind the stern.

"It would be better if we were a little further in," said Rose. Allnutt went in among the reeds again.

This time it was enough. The 'African Queen' lay in thick reeds. At her stern there was a thick line of reeds which had stood up again and made her safe from being seen even if the 'Louisa' came up the channel; and that did not seem at all probable.

Standing up on the edge of the boat Rose and Allnutt could just see over the reeds. The 'Louisa' was going straight on, about a mile from the shore. She was nearly opposite the mouth of the channel now and showed no sign of turning. They watched her for five minutes. She looked beautiful in her white paint against the bright blue of the water. There was the German flag at her stern. In the bow they could just see the gun which gave her command over the Lake. No Arab boat could come into the Lake unless the 'Louisa' allowed.

She was past the channel now and going to the south. There was no more danger of being discovered: she was just making a regular journey

The 'Louisa' was going straight on

round the Lake to make sure that everything was all right.

Rose watched her go, then sat down heavily in the stern of the boat.

"My malaria has started again," she said.

Allnutt did what he could to help her.

"Mine has begun too," he said.

Soon both were helpless, feeling icily cold under the hot sun.

Fourteen

PLAN OF ATTACK

The attack of malaria ended in the late afternoon. Rose got up uncertainly on her feet. Allnutt was just coming out of the sleep which follows an attack of malaria.

She stood up and looked out over the reeds. Towards the south she saw the smoke and the ship, a very small white thing, below it. She thought for a moment that the 'Louisa' was still travelling on her old course. Then she knew that this was not true. She had gone out of sight to the south and then turned and begun to come back again. Allnutt came and stood by Rose's side: they watched the 'Louisa' become larger and clearer as she came back along the shore.

Allnutt whispered, "Do you think she's looking for us?"

"No," said Rose. "She is not. She is only keeping

guard along the shore." Rose hoped that this was true, because her task would be impossible if the Germans were looking out for them.

"I hope you are right," said Allnutt. "I think you are."

"She's going a different way now," said Rose suddenly. The 'Louisa' had turned and was going away from the shore.

"Then she's not looking for us," said Allnutt.

They watched her going across the Lake towards the islands just opposite.

"I wonder what she's going to do!" said Allnutt. But it was he who first noticed that she had stopped. "She's anchoring there among the islands for the night . . . . Look!"

The flag had disappeared from the stern.

"Well, there they are and there they'll stop. That's a good place for anchoring among the islands. We'll see them go in the morning."

He got down, but Rose still stood there. The sun had set. The sky was bright with red and gold. It was already too dark to see the 'Louisa'. "Why must we wait?" she thought. "We must make ready, and plan and strike our blow for England."

"We ought to have been ready for them today," she said to Allnutt: she could just see the red end of his cigarette in the darkness.

"It's all right," said Allnutt. "They'll come again. You know what these Germans are: they make exact rules and keep to them: on Monday they are at one place, on Tuesday some other place. On Wednesday perhaps they are here. I don't know what day it is today. On Sunday I expect they go to Port Livingstone and stay there over Sunday. Then they start again on the same round on Monday."

What Allnutt said agreed with what Rose had seen of the Germans.

"Up at the mine," said Allnutt, "Kaufman, the man in charge there, had to see that everything at the mine was being done right. Their rules were of no use! Kaufman used to come once a week, regularly. The Belgians always knew when he was coming and they had everything ready for him. He would come, look round, have a drink and go. It used to make me laugh."

"Yes, I remember how angry Samuel used to get with their fixed rules."

There was no doubt that, if the 'Louisa' had once anchored among those islands, she would do this again. So Rose's plan was formed: she knew what she must do.

"Charlie," she said, and her voice was gentle.

"Yes, Rose?"

"You must start getting those torpedoes ready. Start tomorrow morning as soon as it is light. How long will it take?"

"I can get the explosive into the tubes quite quickly. But I don't know about the detonators. I've got to make them. It might take two days. I haven't thought about them carefully yet. We've got to cut those holes in the bow: that won't take long. We might have it all done in two days, if we don't get malaria. It depends on the detonators."

"All right."

There was something strange about Rose's voice.

"Rosie, dear," said Allnutt. "Rosie."

"Yes, dear?"

"I know what you are thinking about doing. You needn't try to hide it from me."

Allnutt's voice was very gentle. He took her hand in the darkness.

"You needn't hide it, dear; not now," he said.

"You want to take the 'African Queen' out at night next time the 'Louisa' is here, don't you? Don't you, dear?"

"Yes."

"I think it is the best chance we've got. We ought to be able to do it," said Allnutt.

Allnutt was silent for a few moments. Then he spoke: "You need not come, dear. There's no need for us both to go. I can do it myself, easily."

"Of course not," said Rose. "That wouldn't be right. It's you who ought to stay behind. I can get the launch as far as those islands. I can do that alone. That's what I was meaning to do."

"I know," said Allnutt. "I know that was what you meant to do. But I ought to do that. That's my work. Besides, with those Germans . . ."

So they went on talking. Allnutt was quite prepared to throw away the life which had seemed so precious to him. Rose's plan had become real to him, a task, like a piece of machinery which he must finish. It would be wrong to leave it incomplete. And the sight of the 'Louisa' sailing proudly about the Lake made him angry. He would do anything to stop that! Sailing about the Lake as if they owned it! They should soon see!

They had both agreed to give up their earlier plan of sending the 'African Queen' empty out on her last journey. Rose knew too much about the launch and her uncertain behaviour by now: she wouldn't trust her.

"Well," said Allnutt, "I'll jump off the stern just before she hits. I'll jump off as soon as I'm sure that she will hit the 'Louisa'. I'd be at the stern and the explosion up in the bow wouldn't hurt me." – Of course he knew what two hundred pounds of explosive would really do, and he thought that Rose would not know. But then he saw that the easier and safer he made the task seem, the easier it was for Rose to say, 'If it's so safe and easy, I can do it.'

In the end they decided that they would both go. Certainly they would be more sure of success if one person steered and the other attended to the engine. They also decided that when they were fifty yards from the 'Louisa' one of them would jump over the side. (Allnutt thought that Rose would jump, and Rose thought that it would be Allnutt.)

"Only a week from now," said Allnutt.

Rose stood up in the darkness and looked over the reeds across the Lake. There were stars above, and stars shining below in the water. The moon had not yet risen. But over there were faint lights which were not stars. She pressed Allnutt's arm.

"That's them, all right," said Allnutt.

"But," thought Rose, "if they hide all those lights when they are anchored, it would be impossible to find them. . . . But why should they do that? They are in the only ship on the Lake: that's what they think – forty miles away from their nearest enemy, and that enemy is on land. There would be no need for them to do it."

The sight of those lights made their success quite certain.

Fifteen

TORPEDOES

In the morning the 'Louisa' sailed away to the north on her endless journey round the Lake, keeping guard.

"We'll be ready for her when she comes back," said Rose.

"Yes," said Allnutt.

With Rose's help he took the two heavy gas cylinders from the bottom of the boat and moved them back into the middle. Allnutt opened them and let out the gas with a loud hissing sound. Then he took out the top part of each cylinder, leaving a round hole.

They opened the boxes of explosive very carefully. The explosive was in short round packages of yellow oiled paper. Allnutt began to put them carefully into the cylinders, reaching his arm far down into the inside.

"It would be better if they were all pressed close together in a mass. What can I pack them with?"

He looked round for some packing material.

"Ah! Mud! That's the stuff!"

He went up into the bow and got handfuls of black mud from the bottom of the channel. He put this down in the launch to become nearly dry in the sun.

"I'll do that," said Rose as soon as she saw what he meant to do.

She pressed the water from the black mud and spread it out and worked on it till it was nearly hard. Then she carried it back to Allnutt and set herself to preparing more.

Bit by bit Allnutt filled the cylinders, fixing all the packages of explosive hard and firm with mud. When both the cylinders were full up to the neck he stood up and rubbed his painful back.

"That's done properly," he said with pride.

"Yes," said Rose. They stood looking at the dangerous things as if they had just finished any usual everyday task.

"We've got to make the detonators now," said Allnutt. "I've got an idea. I thought of it last night."

He brought out a gun from his box. It was carefully covered with oil to protect it from the air.

Rose was very surprised: it was the first time she had learned of it.

Allnutt explained: "I had to have this. I sometimes had a lot of gold on the launch going up to Limbasi. But I never had to shoot anyone."

"I'm glad you didn't," said Rose. To shoot a thief in time of peace seemed a much more unpleasant thing than to blow up a whole ship in time of war.

Allnutt opened it and took out the *cartridges*.

"Now, let me think . . . . " he said.

Rose watched Allnutt's work as it took shape under his hands. Meals and sleep and malaria made the task longer. It was two whole days before it was finished.

First he cut out with his knife two round pieces of hard wood which would fit into the noses of the cylinders. Then he made three holes in each piece: the holes were just so big that he could force cartridges into them. The cartridges pointed inwards towards the explosive.

The next part of the work was much more difficult: Allnutt had several failures before he was satisfied. He cut two more pieces of wood of the same size as the first two, but he was very careful about the sort of wood which he chose. It must be neither too hard nor too soft. It must be wood through which a nail could be driven easily, but which would hold the nail firmly. He drove nails into several pieces of wood before at last he decided to use a piece of one of the floor-boards.

Rose did not quite understand the idea. Allnutt worked in the hot sunlight with a cloud of insects round him. Rose sat and watched and gave him things which he asked for.

Allnutt put the second pieces of wood on the others and marked carefully where the bottoms of the cartridges would rest against them. Then he drove nails through the new pieces just at the points which he had marked. Then he fixed the two pieces together – one pair for each cylinder. On one side

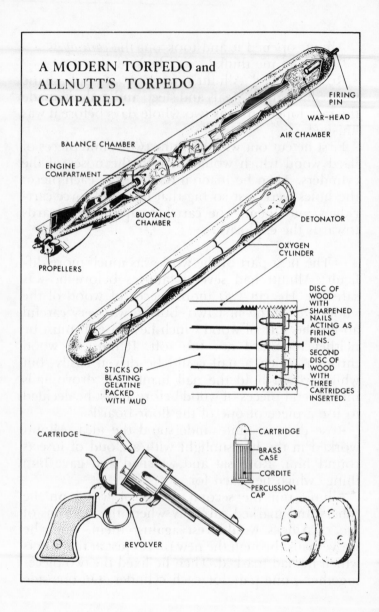

A MODERN TORPEDO and ALLNUTT'S TORPEDO COMPARED.

FIRING PIN

WAR-HEAD

AIR CHAMBER

BALANCE CHAMBER

ENGINE COMPARTMENT

BUOYANCY CHAMBER

DETONATOR

PROPELLERS

OXYGEN CYLINDER

DISC OF WOOD WITH SHARPENED NAILS ACTING AS FIRING PINS.

SECOND DISC OF WOOD WITH THREE CARTRIDGES INSERTED.

STICKS OF BLASTING GELATINE PACKED WITH MUD

CARTRIDGE

CARTRIDGE

BRASS CASE

CORDITE

PERCUSSION CAP

REVOLVER

there were the heads of nails whose points touched the bottoms of the cartridges; and on the other side the cartridges pointed towards the inside of the cylinder. These things would be fixed in the top of each cylinder. The cylinders would point out beyond the bow of the 'African Queen'. The launch would be driven at full speed against the side of the 'Louisa'. Then the nails would be driven in against the cartridges and this would explode the explosives packed in the cylinders.

"That's all right now," said Allnutt. "I don't think I could do it any better. They ought to work all right."

There were three cartridges for each cylinder. At least one ought to explode. There were two cylinders; even one would destroy a little ship like the 'Louisa'.

"Yes," said Rose. "They ought to work all right." They spoke seriously like children talking about some plaything.

"We can't put them in the cylinders now," said Allnutt. "They're dangerous. We had better get the cylinders in place and leave the detonators until we are ready to start."

Rose had a picture in her mind of that starting out. It would certainly be dangerous to push the 'African Queen' out from the reeds in the darkness with two torpedoes in the bow which would explode at a touch.

"We'll put the detonators in after we have got clear of the reeds," he said.

"Yes," said Rose. "Of course it will be dark then.

Will you be able to do it in the dark?"

"I'll have to do it in the dark," said Allnutt. "Yes – I can do it all right."

Allnutt put the detonators away very carefully in the box, and then began to think out the rest of the preparations necessary.

"We must make the holes in the launch for those cylinders. They must be low down, just above the water."

It was very hard work. When it was finished Rose and Allnutt pulled the cylinders into the bow and pushed them forward into the holes until their noses were a foot in front of any part of the boat. Allnutt filled the edges with bits of wool and cloth. He fixed them down very firmly and heaped everything he could on top of them so that the explosive might go forward into the side of the 'Louisa', not upwards. Then he sat down.

"Well, Rose," he said. "We've done it all now. Everything! We're all ready."

It was a great moment – the end of all they had done, their descent of the rapids, their escape at Shona, the repair of the propeller, their battle with the reeds and the water-lilies and the mangroves. The completion of all their task was near.

"Coo!" said Allnutt thinking it over. "Haven't we had a time! Quite a holiday!"

They had done the work so quickly that now they had to suffer a long wait. They had been hard at work ever since the Great Silence – which both now wished to forget, and now they had nothing to do! They had an empty feeling as they thought of those

empty days ahead, even though those days were to
be their last days on earth.

Allnutt felt like a man in prison waiting for the
day when he was to be hanged. He was afraid and
turned to Rose for comfort, and she understood
and was able to calm his fears. There was the fear
that they might begin to hate each other as they
waited there in the reeds as in a grave. They felt
the danger and fought against it.

The storms helped them to fight against this
danger. There were black clouds and wind, and the
Lake was covered with white waves so that even the
'African Queen' was moved by them among the
reeds.

To pass the time they cleaned and worked on the
engine so as to make it quite certain that it would
run properly on its last journey. Allnutt went down
into the mud below the boat to feel if the propeller and shaft were all right. Every few minutes
one or other got up on the edge of the boat to look
out over the reeds and see if the 'Louisa' was in
sight. They saw two African boats, but that was all.
they even began to doubt if the 'Louisa' would ever
come back to that place where she had anchored
before. In black moments they began to doubt if
they would ever succeed.

Then, one morning they looked out over the
reeds and saw her just as before – smoke and a little
white thing below it – coming down from the north.
Just as before she went to the south and disappeared. The slow hours of doubt passed and at last
in the afternoon they saw the smoke coming back,

and they were sure that she would anchor again among the islands. Allnutt was right about the regular ways of the Germans.

Rose and Allnutt watched the 'Louisa' come back from her journey to the south and turn towards the islands, and then stop at the place where she had anchored before. They had talked about a certain question earlier in the week and found no answer. Now they knew the answer. They had just turned away from looking at the 'Louisa': they were just going to make their preparations to start: then they stood holding each other's hands and looking into each other's eyes. Each knew what the other was thinking.

"Rosie, dear," said Allnutt, "we're going out together, aren't we?"

"Yes, dear," she said. "I should like it that way."

Now that they had to decide, they had decided without difficulty. They would stand side by side with equal chance of living when the 'African Queen' drove her torpedoes against the side of the 'Louisa'. They could not bear the thought of being parted now.

It was almost dark. The young moon was low in the sky: soon there would be only the stars to give them light.

"It's safe for us to get ready now," said Rose.

"Goodbye, dear."

"Goodbye, dearest," said Allnutt.

Their preparations took a long time. They had expected this, but they had the whole night before them. The best time to reach the 'Louisa' would be in the early hours of the morning because their attack must be a surprise.

Allnutt had to go down into the mud and water and cut away the reeds round the stern of the 'African Queen' so that they might pass out easily into the channel.

When they were in the river Allnutt tied the boat to some reeds. Then he took the detonators out of the box and went down into the water at the bow. He was a long time there standing in mud and deep water while he fixed the detonators into the noses of the cylinders. It was a difficult task and took a long time. The 'African Queen' was moving a little in the waves coming from the Lake: they made it still more difficult. Rose stood in the bow to help him. If his hand hit the heads of those nails they would both be blown to bits; and the 'Louisa' would still rule the Lake.

It was very dark. Rose could just see him move away from the torpedoes and come round at a safe distance from them. His hands reached up and he pulled himself into the boat.

"I've done it," he whispered. Then he put up the funnel again: this made a faint noise. It all took time.

The fire below the boiler was all ready: he had only to light it .... Bright burning bits of wood came up out of the funnel.

"They'll see that!" Rose whispered.

"It's all right," Allnutt whispered in reply. "I'll see that it doesn't happen when we are getting close to them."

The engine was moving now, sending hissing steam out of its joints – *ss . . . ss . . . ss*. Then Allnutt untied the rope and took the boat-hook. He pushed the launch out into the middle of the river: he put down the boat-hook and opened the steam pipe. The propeller began to turn. Rose stood at the tiller and steered them out of the river towards the Lake. They were starting now to "strike a blow for England".

The 'African Queen' came out from the river into the Lake. They had passed through such difficulties and dangers to do this and now the end was in sight. The two torpedoes pointed out through the bow: a touch could explode them. Rose, standing in the stern, could just see the little light which showed where the 'Louisa' was. There were no stars above them.

In daylight they would have seen the dark clouds gathering in the sky and they would have felt that wet heaviness of the air. They did not know that this north wind told of a coming storm: and they did not know how quickly this north wind coming down from the mountains could beat up the waves of the Lake to madness.

Rose felt the movement of the launch as the waves became bigger and fiercer. She did not know that the 'African Queen' was not built to deal with rough water: the sides were low flat walls, and the bottom was flat. Waves struck the flat sides and the tops of them came in. Rose thought that this was to be expected in open water. She felt no fear.

The wind dropped for a moment, but the water

was still rough. Then the rain came like a river from the sky. The wind raised the waves of the Lake into mountains. The bow of the 'African Queen' came up out of the water then went down again with a crash.

It was dark – black darkness. All Rose could do was to keep her hand on the tiller and try to remain standing. There was no chance of seeing the lights of the 'Louisa'.

Allnutt was at her side. He was putting her arm through the one *life-buoy*[1] which the 'African Queen' carried. Then, as they stood together there, a wave carried him away. She tried to call him. Then she felt water come up round her. A wave struck her face. It was hard to breathe: there was water in her nose.

The life of the 'African Queen' was finished. She had gone down to the bottom of the Lake. Her brave attempt to torpedo the 'Louisa' had ended. And, as it ended, the storm ended too. The storm died away as if it had been raised just to help the Germans and protect their ship.

Sixteen

ON THE 'LOUISA'

The Captain of the 'Louisa' looked at this very strange-looking prisoner. He tried not to see him as he was now, but as he might have looked in his

[1] *Life-buoy* = a circle made of material which holds up a man in the water.

usual clothes. The man's hair was long and dirty; he had the rough beginnings of a beard; but the face was the sort of face one might see any day in the streets of Berlin. The prisoner was a very sick man: he was tired out; he seemed to have lost hope, and he was very ill. It was quite clear that he had malaria. The prisoner's clothes added to his curious appearance. The Captain sat back in his chair: "He may be mad; but this is not a simple case of spying – trying to find out our movements so as to help the British. No: he is not just a spy. A spy would be hanged. There must be something to be said in his defence."

Lieutenant Schmidt gave the facts against the prisoner: "The prisoner was seen on the island Prince Eitel at daylight. He was immediately hunted down and made a prisoner. He could not – or would not – tell anything about himself. Stores of oil are kept on that island which an enemy could very easily destroy. The island also gives many chances of watching the movements of the 'Louisa'. He was found in a place forbidden by General von Hanneken to everyone except the members of the German Army. As he is not German he has no right to be where he was found and must therefore be hanged."

"There is no need," thought the Captain, "for this Lieutenant to tell me what I must or ought to do. Perhaps he will be telling me, next, that I am the Captain of the 'Louisa'." He turned to Lieutenant Schumann who had been ordered to defend the prisoner.

Lieutenant Schumann was old and not very bright. The Captain had to choose him for the task because of the six officers on the 'Louisa' one was keeping watch above, and one was in the engine-room and two were acting as judges in the court. Only old Schumann was left for the defence. He said a few words, then stopped. He was not good at public speaking.

The Captain looked at the prisoner, expecting him to speak.

Allnutt was too tired and too ill to notice much. He knew that this was some sort of court and that he was being tried as a prisoner. He did not know what he was being tried for – for doing what? He did not know what the judgment might be. He didn't care: "Nothing matters now," he thought. "I've lost Rosie and the 'African Queen' is down at the bottom of the Lake, and our great attempt has ended. I'm ill and I almost wish I were dead."

He looked at the Captain and the two Lieutenants.

"They are expecting me to say something," he thought. "But it's too much trouble, and they would not understand."

The Captain knew that it was his duty to discover if anything could be said in defence of the prisoner.

"What are you? Are you Belgian or English?"

The Captain spoke in German but Allnutt understood the word 'English'.

"English," he said. "British."

"Your name?" asked the Captain in German. Then trying to remember his English he repeated the question: "What – is – your – name?"

"Charles Allnutt."

It took a long time to write this down as Allnutt

gave the English names of the letters.

"What were you doing on the island?" asked the Captain in German. He was not surprised that the prisoner did not understand him. Then he thought: "He may speak Swahili." Swahili is the mixed language spoken by the peoples of East and Central Africa. The seamen on the 'Louisa' spoke Swahili. He repeated the question in Swahili: "What were you doing on the island?"

"Nothing," said Allnutt. He wasn't going to tell them about the 'African Queen': it would be wiser not to do that.

The Captain asked him again.

"Nothing," he said. ". . . . Nothing."

The Captain did not know what else he could do. He supposed that the man must be hanged. He had ordered the death of only one man before this – that man was half-Arab, half-European, and he was hanged at the side of the Lake to give a lesson to other spies; but bodies did not last long in this heat.

At this moment there was a noise outside. The door opened and an African seaman came in pulling another prisoner after him. At the sight of her the Captain stood up, for the prisoner was a woman. She was a white woman although her skin was burnt brown by the sun. There was a mass of brown hair hanging over her face.

"She was found on one of the other islands. We found this also," said the man in Swahili. He showed a life-buoy. They could see the name 'African Queen' on the life-buoy.

" 'African Queen'?" said the Captain trying to remember something about the name. He searched through a mass of papers till he found what he wanted. It was a notice sent out by von Hanneken. Until that moment the news of the missing launch on the Upper Ulanga river had been of no interest to the Captain of the 'Louisa'. But now it was different!

He looked at the new prisoner. She was trying to hold her clothes together.

"Lieutenant Schmidt, give her a coat," he said.

The officer brought a coat.

"A chair!" said the Captain.

The officer gave her his chair.

The Captain knew who these people must be. The man was the engineer of the 'African Queen', and the woman must be the sister of the missionary. They must have left the 'African Queen' in the Upper Ulanga river and come down in a small boat, and last night when the storm came they were trying to cross the Lake so as to get to the Belgian Congo.

"And now, dear lady . . . ." said the Captain.

He began to question Rose in Swahili. He found that she also knew a little German. Samuel had taught her German from a book; she had found it very difficult and did not learn much.

Then the Captain discovered that Allnutt and Rose had brought the 'African Queen' down the rapids of the Ulanga river into the Lake.

"But, dear lady . . . ." said the Captain, "it was very dangerous." The Captain had read the book written by Spengler, the only man who had travelled

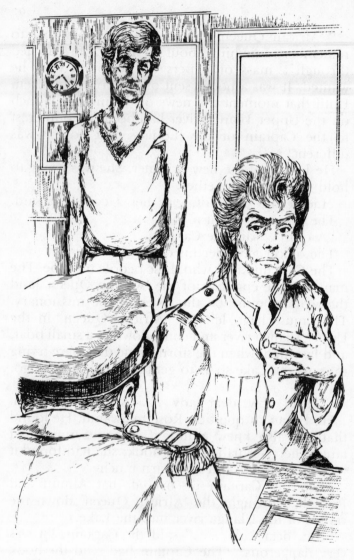

The Captain began to question Rose

the whole length of the river; but he did that in a small African boat.

Rose did not answer. It did not matter. "Nothing matters now," she thought. She was glad to see Allnutt there, but even her love for him seemed to be dead, now that the 'African Queen' was lost and 'Louisa' still ruled the Lake.

The Captain had heard about the bravery of English women. Their power of suffering pain without complaining and their calmness in danger. Here he had clear proof.

There was now no question of spying nor of death. He could not hang one person without the other, and he had not thought for a moment of hanging Rose. Even if she was a spy, he would not hang her. And, beside that, she had brought a steam launch from the Upper Ulanga river to the Lake. As a seaman he could hardly believe it: yet it was a fact. It was wonderful!

"But why," he asked, "did not your friend here tell us?"

Rose looked round at Allnutt, and saw how ill he was – hardly able to stand. All her feelings as a woman came back to her. She got up from her chair and went to him, to protect him.

"He is ill and tired," she said, angrily. "He ought to be in bed."

She put her arm round him while she struggled to say in German and Swahili just what she thought of men who could treat a poor creature in that way. She put her hand against his face and whispered words of love to him. She, too, had malaria, but in the white coat of a German officer she looked a fine woman.

"But you are ill too," said the Captain.

Rose did not trouble to answer him.

The Captain looked round at the members of the Court. "You may go," he said.

As the four officers left the room he tried to decide on his future action. Of course these two ought to be put in the Prisoners' Camp: that is what von Hanneken would do if he took them away. But they were ill and they might die if they were put in a prisoners' camp. He thought, "It isn't right that two people who have done so much should die as prisoners. In German Central Africa prisoners are not treated well. What difference would one sick man and one sick woman make in a war between two nations? Von Hanneken would be very angry if he knew, but I am the Captain of the 'Louisa' and my own master on the Lake. I can do what I choose in my own ship."

The Captain had decided what he would do almost before Schumann shut the door.

Seventeen

HANDED OVER TO THE BRITISH

Port Albert is a town in the Belgian Congo on the shore of the Lake. The officer in command there was British. He was walking about seeing to the preparation of two boats which had been sent to attack the 'Louisa'. They had been sent from England and brought to Port Albert with great difficulty by rail and river.

They were very small, but very fast - four times as fast as the 'Louisa', and each had a gun which fired twice as quickly as the old gun on the 'Louisa'. The Commander was eager to get on with his task: the sooner he could get these boats out, hunting for the 'Louisa', the better.

He looked out over the Lake and stopped suddenly. He could see smoke far away, and a small white thing below the smoke. An officer came running along to him: he had glasses in his hand. He offered them to the Commander: "Look, sir," he said. "That's the 'Louisa'."

The Commander looked through the glasses. "Yes," he said. "She looks as if she was ready for battle; but what's that flag she's flying? That isn't a German flag. It's . . . what do you think it is?"

The officer looked through the glasses.

"I think . . . ." he said. "Yes: it's a white flag."

"I think so too," said the Commander. "I wonder what they mean to do. Surely they aren't going to come in close under the white flag and then attack us?"

The Commander ran up to the top of the hill above Port Albert. There was a Belgian officer there, and two guns.

"If they are planning some trick they'll be sorry. We can hit them with these guns," said the Commander.

But the Germans did not seem to be thinking of making any attack. The 'Louisa' turned sideways to the shore much too far away for her gun to hit anything. Then the Commander saw white smoke and heard the bang of a gun, and saw the white flag come halfway down and then go up again.

"That means that they want a "parley" – they want to talk to us."

It was not his way to send others into danger.

"I'll go," he said. Then he turned to the young officer. "You stay here. You are in command while I'm out there. If you see any need to fire, fire as fast as you can. Don't mind me. Do you understand?"

"Yes, sir."

"I'll have to go in one of these African boats," he said. A number of them had been lying there for months for fear of the 'Louisa', and now they were used to hide the work which was being done on the two British ships.

The young officer watched through his glasses as the boat went out from the shore. The Commander sitting in the stern was wearing a plain white coat. The officer watched him steer towards the 'Louisa' far out on the Lake. Soon all he could see of the boat was its yellow sail. He saw it reach the 'Louisa', then disappear as the sail was taken in and the boat came to the side of the 'Louisa'.

There was an anxious delay; at last the yellow sail was seen again; she was coming back. Another gun was fired as the 'Louisa' turned away and went back again towards the German shore.

The 'Louisa' was now so far away that she could hardly be seen, but the African boat was close to the shore. The young officer left his post and went down to meet the Commander. The boat came quickly in; the African seaman took in the sail. The Commander was there sitting in the stern, and there were two people lying in the bottom of the boat. The officer looked at them in surprise; one was a woman. She had a dress made of sail-cloth with coloured lines on it: once it had been part of an awning on the 'Louisa'; and above that she had a white coat with gold on it showing that it had once belonged to a German officer. The young officer hardly looked at the other person in the boat because he was so surprised at the sight of a woman; but the other person was dressed in the clothes of an African seaman on a German ship.

"Get some men to carry these people," said the Commander. "They're very ill."

Both of them were having a bad attack of malaria, so bad that they hardly knew where they were. The officer had them carried up onto the shore, then he looked round to see what he could do with them. In the end he put them in one of the tents used by the English seamen; that was the only place where he could put them, because in Port Albert there was nothing but African huts.

"They'll be all right in an hour or two," said the doctor after examining them.

"I don't know what I'm going to   with them!" said the Commander. "This isn't a place for a sick woman."

"Who is she?" asked the young officer.

"Some missionary woman. The 'Louisa' found her somewhere on the Lake trying to escape over to here."

"It's very good of the Germans to bring them over."

"Yes," said the Commander shortly.

"They may be able to tell us something useful about the Germans," said the officer.

"Can we ask them?" asked the Doctor. "If they were brought in under a white flag, I don't know if we ought to."

"Oh, yes, you can ask them all right," said the Commander. "There is nothing against that, but you won't learn anything useful from them."

When the Commander came to question Rose and Allnutt about the Germans, he found that they had very little to tell them: indeed they could tell him nothing that he did not know already.

The Commander thought for a moment of the battle which would decide the mastery of the Lake, and then of the future when African boats, guarded by his two ships, would take over the army which would put a final end to von Hanneken. He asked if the Germans had made any preparations to prevent the British from landing on their shore of the Lake.

"I didn't see anything," said Allnutt.

Rose understood the meaning of the question better.

"You can't land anyone in the place where we came from; it is all mud and water-lilies and reeds and malaria."

"No," said the Commander. "I don't think I could land there, if it's like that. How did you get down to the Lake then?"

"We came down the Ulanga river," said Rose.

"Really?"

The Commander was not very interested. "I didn't know that was possible," he said.

"It isn't. Cor! It isn't," said Allnutt.

"That's interesting," said the Commander, but he didn't sound interested. "You must let me hear about it later on."

He could hardly be expected to be interested in the doings of two very ordinary people who had foolishly lost their boat. Tomorrow he had to lead his ships against the 'Louisa', and he had much to think about.

"They may be all right," he said when he came away. "They seem to be all right; but they may not be. All this may be just a trick of von Hanneken to get two of his friends over here. I wouldn't be surprised if it were so. They must not come out of their tents until the 'Louisa' is sunk. They do not seem to be married, but, although they have lived together all these weeks, it wouldn't be right to put them in a tent together. I can't really spare another tent and I've got to take a man off work to stand guard over them. You see to it, will you? I must go and have a look at the 'Matilda's' gun."

Eighteen

BATTLE

The next morning the Captain of the 'Louisa' saw two long grey shapes cutting through the water and throwing up high waves on each side of their bows as they came towards him. He could see on them the flags of British fighting ships.

"Action!" he shouted. "Get that gun firing!"

Lieutenant Schmidt ran madly to the gun and Lieutenant Schumann went to the wheel to stand by the African seamen and make sure that the Captain's orders were obeyed.

The 'Louisa' came round to face her enemies. Her gun spoke – once – twice, very slowly. The 'Matilda' and the 'Amelia' turned to one side. Then they came rushing round in a wide circle just too far away for the 'Louisa's' gun to hit them. The 'Louisa' was slow in movement and she could not turn quickly enough to keep her bow pointing towards those flying grey shapes which came nearer and nearer. They had four times the speed of the German ship and were ten times quicker in turning. Lieutenant Schmidt tried to aim his gun, but could only see the boiling water behind them. He could not turn his gun any further round and the ship could not turn any faster.

The British Commander stood in the 'Matilda'.
He looked calmly at the lessening distance between
him and the 'Louisa'. His course was bringing him
quickly to the stern of the enemy where there was
no gun. He must not only win easily, but he must
see that the battle was won at the smallest cost.
He looked back to see that the 'Amelia' was in her
correct place. He shouted an order into the ear of
the man at the wheel and then waved his hand to
the officer in the bow near the gun. The gun began
firing rapidly, shot after shot.

The shots from the 'Matilda' began to strike
the stern of the 'Louisa'. At first they only blew
holes in the sides; but soon they went through into
the middle of the ship bringing fire and destruction
everywhere.

It was no longer possible to steer the 'Louisa'.
She turned back suddenly from her course and
went on in a straight line. The Commander in the
'Matilda' gave a new order and kept his boats
behind her, and from there sent shot after shot
through and through the ship from stern to bow.

The boiler was hit and the 'Louisa' was hidden
in a cloud of steam. The men in her engine room
were boiled alive.

The Commander in the 'Matilda' had been expecting that moment. When he saw the steam he gave
a quick order; the 'Matilda's' engine stopped.
When the steam cleared away the 'Louisa' was lying
helplessly on the water and the two British ships
were lying silent, still safely at her stern.

The battle was over; but the German flag was

still flying; they were still fighting. Something hit the water beside the 'Matilda' and the Commander could hear a noise from the 'Louisa': some men were firing at them with *rifles*.[1] Even at the distance of a mile and a half a rifle shot can kill, and the Commander must not let his seamen be in any more danger than was necessary.

He did not want to kill the Germans who were carrying on this useless defence; but he must do what was necessary.

"All right then!" he said.

He shouted an order and his gun began firing again. It fired a little higher. One shot killed three seamen who were lying there firing their rifles. Lieutenant Schmidt never knew how he escaped. Another shot killed Lieutenant Schumann. But the Captain was not hit: he had gone down below just before, holding his coat over his face because of the hot steam in the engine-room. He had gone to do his last task.

"Perhaps that will finish them," said the Commander ordering his gun to cease firing. He looked at the 'Louisa' again. She lay there without movement covered with smoke and steam. There was no firing now, but the German flag was still flying.

Then the Commander saw that she was lower in the water, and, as he watched, the 'Louisa' suddenly fell over on one side. The German Captain had done his last task. He had opened the *sea-cocks*.[2] The 'Louisa' went down to the bottom of the Lake.

---

[1] *rifles* = small guns such as soldiers carry.

[2] *sea-cocks* = pipes which let the water into the ship.

"I hope we can save the poor fellows," said the Commander.

The 'Matilda' and the 'Amelia' came rushing up just as the German flag went down into the water. They were in time to save all those who were still living.

Nineteen

THE END

The wounded men were carried carefully along the shore to be taken care of by the doctor.

A report of the victory had to be written and sent to London, and another report written in French had to be sent by the Belgian Commander to Brussels.

The Commander's mind was already hard at work on his future plans for the time when he could lead his army across the Lake against von Hanneken. This must be done as soon as possible, before von Hanneken had time to deal with this unexpected loss of the 'Louisa' and make arrangements to fight against a landing.

The Commander had other things to think of, things which must be dealt with now. He had some wounded German prisoners and some unwounded prisoners. He must deal with them at once. He sent for Rose and Allnutt.

"I am sending some German prisoners down to

the coast," he said. "I'm going to send you with them. Will that be all right for you?"

"I suppose so," said Allnutt. Until this moment he and Rose had been people without a future. Even the destruction of the 'Louisa' had given them a feeling that there was nothing in front of them, nothing in their future.

"You'll join the army, I suppose?" said the Commander. "I can't arrange for that here but down on the coast you will find a British *Consul* at Matardi."

"A Consul?" said Allnutt.

"Yes, an Officer of the British government who can deal with you. Any British Consul can do your business for you. Of course that will be as soon as you are well and strong again. He will send you round to join the South African army; so you will be all right."

"Yes, sir," said Allnutt.

"And you, Mrs – er – Miss Sayer, isn't it?" said the Commander. "I think the coast is the best place for you too, you can get back to England from there, a British Consul . . . ."

"Yes," said Rose.

"That will be all right then," said the Commander. "You will be starting in two or three hours."

"Mrs – er – Miss." The Commander had said "Mrs – er – Miss." Those words really settled Rose's future. When they came out from the Commander's room Rose felt deeply ashamed. Until then she had been a woman without a future and so had no troubles to care about. It was different now.

The Commander had said that she might go back to England. To Rose this meant a picture of poor streets and the members of her family all asking questions. The family always asked questions. And she would be separated from Allnutt. He had been so much to her: he had hardly been out of her sight for weeks now: to lose him now would be like losing an arm or a leg. Even if her feelings towards him had changed: she could not think of this future of hers without Allnutt.

"Charlie," she said, "we've got to get married."

"Coo!" said Allnutt. This was something that he had not really thought of.

"We must do it as quickly as we can," said Rose. "A Consul can marry people. That officer in there spoke about a Consul. As soon as we get to the coast ———"

Allnutt didn't know what to say, this sudden journey to the coast, and the idea of joining the army, and now this new question left him with hardly a word to say. "Rose is so much above me," he thought. "I'm just a working man, and she's – she's middle-class. And then there's money. I suppose I'll get pay in the army."

"All right, Rosie," he said. "Let's get married."

So they left the Lake and began the long journey to Matardi – and to marriage.

Did they live happily ever after? It is difficult to say.

112

QUESTIONS

Chapter **1**

1. What is the date of this book?
2. In what part of Africa did Rose Sayer and her brother Samuel work?
3. What were they?
4. Samuel was very ———. What?
5. What had General von Hanneken taken away?—"Everything except ———."

1. What were Samuel's last words?
2. How old was Rose?
3. How long had she been in Africa?
4. What did she feel about the Germans?

1. What did Rose want to do?
2. Who was Rose's "chance"?
3. Where was this man employed?—"At the———, ——— miles up the river."

Chapter **2**

1. Rose said "Look!". What did Allnutt see?
2. What is a launch?
3. What is Blasting Gelatine?
4. (a) What are cylinders?
   (b) What was in the cylinders?

1. What will Allnutt do?
2. What did Allnutt ask Rose to do?
3. Where was the launch?

1. How long was the launch?
2. What are the "bows" of a ship?
3. What is the stern?
4. What do you have under an awning?
5. Draw a picture of the ship and mark the Funnel, Engine, Propeller, Tiller, Anchor.
6. What is a tiller used for? For ———ing a boat.

1. Where did the boat go?
2. What came out from the bushes?
3. What is gin?
4. Allnutt had no idea of ———. Of doing what?

1. What was the 'Louisa'?
2. What does Allnutt call the 'Louisa'?
3. Why could not the British get at von Hanneken?
4. What did Rose say?—"We must ———."

1. What was Allnutt's idea?—"To be ——."
2. Why can't they go down the river into the Lake? "Because of the ——."
3. How did Spengler get down the river?
4. How did the launch come to the river?—"By ——."
5. How was the 'Louisa' brought to the Lake?

1. What did women of Rose's class do?
2. (a) What did Rose feel as she came out to Africa?
   (b) What did she feel proud of?
3. How do you explode Blasting Gelatine?—"With a ——."

1. What do warships do with torpedoes?—"They send —— to ——."
2. How will Rose make a torpedo? "Put —(a)— inside the —(b)—. Push them out —(c)—; then run the launch against —(d)—."
3. What would the torpedo do to the launch and Rose and Allnutt?
4. What did Rose want to torpedo?

1. What hope would not lead Allnutt into danger?—"The hope of —(a)— and —(b)—.
2. What was Rose's answer to Allnutt's fear?—"We wouldn't be ——."
3. Allnutt said, "We can't do that."—Can't do what?

1. When might Rose see what a silly idea it was to go down the river?—"After going over ——."
2. How far away is the first Rapid?
3. What was Rose expecting to do?
4. How much daylight was left?

1. What had Allnutt got to do again?
2. What did Rose begin to learn?
3. Why did they have to stop?
4. What is a channel?

1. Where must the bow of a boat be pointing when you anchor?
2. What did Allnutt offer to Rose?
3. How many cups of tea used Samuel to drink every day?

1. What did they eat at supper? "—— and ——."
2. Where did Allnutt have a bath?
3. In what did Rose have a bath at the Mission?
4. What did Rose quite calmly think of doing when she came back into the launch?
5. Where did Allnutt sleep?

Chapter **3**

1. What woke Rose?
2. What did she see moving?
3. What did Rose almost do?
4. What had Allnutt learnt to do?

1. What two things must they do before they start?
2. The pump was a ——.
3. What can they do as they go along?

1. What did Allnutt do before he pulled up the anchor?
2. What could not Rose do?— "—— the launch when it was ——."
3. What did Rose not notice when Allnutt brought her breakfast?

1. Rose's mouth was —— and her eyes were ——.
2. (a) Where did Allnutt look anxiously?—At the ——.
   (b) Why?
3. The side-streams were —— places.
4. By what were they sometimes stopped?

1. What had Allnutt to cut away from the propeller?
2. With what did they push the boat forward?
3. What was there at the bottom of the river?
4. What did Rose not know in her mind, but her body told her?—"That she ——."

Chapter 4

1. What did the third drink seem to do?
2. When will they reach the rapids?
3. What will there be at Shona?
4. Why can't they pass Shona at night?

1. Allnutt had no idea of ——. Of doing what?
2. What did Allnutt do when he thought of his mother?
3. Rose decided to make Allnutt ——. What?

1. What did Rose do to the bottles of gin?
2. What did Allnutt do after drinking the water?
3. Rose had breakfast, washed her clothes, sat down. That was the beginning of ——. What?

1. What did Rose begin to do?
2. Why is this a help to a woman?—"Because she is —— and he cannot ——."
3. What did Allnutt do to his hair?

Chapter 5

1. What did Rose take out of her work-bag?
2. Why could not Allnutt bear silence? Because as a child he had ——.
3. Why did Allnutt think there was something seriously wrong with him?

1. What did Allnutt ask Rose? What did Rose answer?
2. Where was Shona?
3. How did the river flow at Shona?
4. What did the Askaris do when they saw the launch?

1. What did the German officer think that Rose and Allnutt would do?
2. How many Askari soldiers came running to the officer?
3. Why was it difficult for the officer to shoot at the launch?

1. Will the officer tell von Hanneken about the 'African Queen'?
2. What did the officer think would happen to the people in the 'African Queen'?
3. Of whom did he think as the third person?

Chapter **6**

1. (a) Where did Rose steer the launch?
   (b) Why?
2. What did two shots hit?
3. (a) Why could not Rose see forward?
   (b) What did she do?

1. What was there lower down, past the first rock?
2. What was there beyond that?
3. What was in Rose's path just beyond the waterfall?
4. What might this do to the launch?
5. What did Allnutt do which he had not done since he left school?

1. What did the river pass through lower down?
2. Then the river looked as if it ——. As if it flowed—where?
3. What sign did Allnutt make? What was he telling her?

1. It seemed as if the 'African Queen' would ——. Would do what?
2. When did the launch go into quiet water?
3. What feelings had Rose? She felt —— and she had a —— —— inside.

1. There were no —(a)— and no fear of —(b)—.
2. The shore was covered with ——. What?
3. What did Allnutt do just before he fell asleep?

Chapter **7**

1. What did Allnutt do when Rose made her second sign?
2. What did the river do towards afternoon?
3. How did the side-stream come into the river?

1. What was in Allnutt's foot?
2. What did Allnutt say when he looked at the flowers?
3. Rose's neck was —— and ——.

Chapter **8**

1. Who prepared the breakfast?
2. What did Rose call Allnutt?
3. What followed the crash?

1. Allnutt prayed that the —— might not ——.
2. What did the propeller seem to do?
3. What was there on the left?
4. Rose had to allow for the —(a)— and this —(b)—.

116

1. The bow was ———. Doing what?
2. What did the water do?
3. Allnutt put his —(a)— under the bow of the launch.
4. What thought still troubled Rose?
5. What did Allnutt say?—"I wonder how much ———."

1. Rose felt that pumping out the boat was like ———. Like what?
2. Was any more water coming into the launch?
3. (a) What was bent?   (b) What was lost?

1. What could Allnutt already see himself and Rose doing?
2. When did Allnutt feel better?—When he had ———.
3. What could not Rose imagine?

1. Rose asked, "Can't we get ——— without ———?
2. Whom did Rose see working on iron?
3. What did Allnutt not believe in?
4. Allnutt said, "It's no use. I was forgetting ———." Forgetting what?

1. What would the propeller do if it had only two blades?
2. What does welding mean?
3. When Allnutt said, "I'll see what I can do", it was just like a loving husband asked to ———. To do what?

1. How much of the broken blade remained?
2. What happened to Allnutt as a result of staying so long in the water?
3. What did Allnutt make?

1. From where did they get more wood?
2. What happened to every piece of clothing?
3. What wish did Allnutt feel for a moment?

1. Allnutt had to make a piece of metal which would fit round ——— and round the ———.
2. What would be the answer if the propeller did not stand up to real work?
3. What did Rose and Allnutt say which neither of them heard?
4. What did not the shaft make?

Chapter **9**

1. What became less below the last rapid?
2. What did the river form?
3. How far ahead had Rose to choose her course?
4. What had they not got now to protect them?

1. What came after the rain?
2. What new sort of fly came?
3. Under what did they sleep?

1. How many journeys did they make to get wood?
2. What did they do when Rose steered near to each mass of plants and branches?
3. What can they use again?
4. What did they eat for supper? (3 things).

Chapter **10**

1. With what was the bank covered?
2. What made it difficult to see the distance?
3. Rose thought that the river must have ——. Have done what?

1. Where did Rose steer the launch?
2. In what way was the water different?
3. How could Rose see that they were going in the opposite direction from when they entered?

1. What did Rose know after ten minutes?—That they had come ——.
2. What did Rose tell Allnutt to do?
3. Why was Rose angry?

1. Rose was not used to ——. What?
2. About what did Allnutt feel very wise?
3. Why did the 'African Queen' stop?
4. How must they make the launch go on?

1. Why was there no wind?
2. After about how long did Allnutt give up the work?
3. How far were they in among the reeds after the first day?
4. What was Rose saying to herself as she fought the flies?

Chapter **11**

1. What came during that night?
2. What noise did Rose hear?
3. In what direction were they going now?

1. What did Allnutt say when he gave a cry of joy?
2. How far did the launch move when Allnutt pulled the boat-hook?
3. With what was the water covered?

1. What did Allnutt feel?—"That the plants were being ——."
2. Rose said, "Can't we try ——. " Try doing what?
3. Why did they cease to move at all?
4. Rose wanted to stop Allnutt from doing ——. Doing what?

1. How much must Rose count before pulling the rope?
2. How many times did Allnutt go down?
3. What things were on Allnutt's body?

1. What did Rose use to get these things off Allnutt's body?
2. Allnutt was nearly ——. Doing what?
3. "What we haven't done yet is to ——." To do what?

Chapter **12**

1. Where could not water-lilies grow?
2. What did Allnutt say when he looked down into the water?
3. What did Allnutt make?

1. How fast did they travel?
2. What things did they take down so as to go under the trees?
3. For what danger had they to look carefully in the half-light?
4. What illness did the insects give them?

1. Why did they eat very little?—Because the food ——
2. All the time they were afraid for ——. For what?
3. They looked more like ——. Like what?

1. Where was the Lake?
2. Why must they stop?—To do what?
3. What had Allnutt not thought about for weeks?

Chapter **13**

1. How many islands were there?
2. How wide, how long was the Lake?
3. What was the next thing which they had to do?

1. What did Rose do that night?
2. What was Allnutt content to do?
3. What did Rose see?

1. What might the 'Louisa' see?—The —— and the ——.
2. In what direction was the 'Louisa' moving?
3. How far into the reeds did they get the launch?

1. How many times did Allnutt go down to cut the reeds?
2. How long did they watch the 'Louisa'?
3. What could they just see on the 'Louisa'?
4. What had started again?

Chapter **14**

1. What had the 'Louisa' done?
2. Was the 'Louisa' looking for the 'African Queen'?
3. Where was the 'Louisa' anchoring?

1. What do the Germans do?
2. Where will the 'Louisa' go on Sunday?
3. How often did Kaufman visit the Belgian mines?

1. What can Allnutt do quickly?
2. What must he make?
3. What does Rose want to do?
4. What does Allnutt say to this?

1. What plan had they given up?—The plan of sending — — —.
2. What did Allnutt say that he would do just as the launch hit the 'Louisa'?
3. What did they decide in the end?
4. What made their success seem certain?

Chapter **15**

1. How was the explosive packed?
2. With what did they press the explosives together?
3. What did Allnutt do when the cylinders were full?

1. What did Allnutt take out of his box?
2. Why did he carry this?—Because he sometimes had a lot of —— in the launch.
3. Where must the pieces of wood fit?
4. What did he force into this thing?

1. What did he put into the second piece of wood?
2. (a) What was on one side of the piece of wood?
   (b) What was on the other side?

1. How many cartridges were there for each cylinder?
2. When will they put the detonators into the cylinders?—When the launch is ——.
3. Where must the holes in the launch be?

1. With what did Allnutt fill the edges?—With —— and ——.
2. What did Allnutt say when they saw that the end of their task was near?
3. There was the fear that they might ——. Might do what?

1. What did they do to pass the time?
2. What boats did they see?
3. Where did the 'Louisa' anchor?
4. Allnutt said, "Rosie dear, we're going out together, aren't we?" What did she answer?

1. What sort of moon was there?
2. When was the best time to reach the 'Louisa'?
3. What did Allnutt do when they were out in the river?
4. What did he do when he got back into the boat?

1. Allnutt said, "I'll see that it doesn't happen when we are getting close."—What must not happen?
2. What could Rose see?
3. What could they not see?

1. In what two ways was the 'African Queen' not built for rough water?
2. Where was Allnutt putting Rose's arm?
3. What happened to Allnutt?

Chapter **16**

1. What added to Allnutt's curious appearance?
2. What would be done to a spy?
3. Where was Allnutt found?
4. What had Lieutenant Schumann been ordered to do?

1. Lieutenant Schumann was not good at ——. At what?
2. What did Allnutt almost wish?
3. What did the Captain ask Allnutt?

1. Why did it take a long time to write Allnutt's name?— "Because Allnutt gave ——."
2. In what language did the Captain speak to Allnutt?
3. How many men had the Captain ordered to be hanged before this?

1. What did the Captain do when Rose was brought in?
2. What did they find with Rose?
3. What did Lieutenant Schmidt give to Rose? (Two things).
4. Why did the Captain think Rose was trying to cross the Lake?

1. What book had the Captain read?

2. What had the Captain heard about?
3. What did Rose do when she looked at Allnutt?—"She went to ——."

1. What sort of coat was Rose wearing?
2. What did the Captain tell the members of the court to do?
3. Where ought Rose and Allnutt to be put?
4. When had the Captain decided what he would do?

Chapter **17**

1. What was the name of the town?
2. What things were being prepared?
3. How fast could the guns fire?
4. What flag was the 'Louisa' flying?

1. What was on the top of the hill?—"A —— and ——".
2. "They want a parley"—What does that mean?
3. How will the Commander go out to the 'Louisa'?
4. What colour was the sail?

1. From what had Rose's dress been made?
2. In what was Allnutt dressed?
3. Where were Rose and Allnutt put?—In one of the —— ——.

1. What were Rose and Allnutt able to tell the Commander?
2. The commander asked if the Germans had done anything to prevent the British from —— ——. From doing what?
3. Why is it not possible to land in the place from which Rose had come? (Four reasons).

1. The Commander said, "I did not know that it was possible to come down the Ulanga river." What did Allnutt answer?
2. When had the Commander got to attack the 'Louisa'?
3. What must the Commander go and look at?

Chapter **18**

1. Where did Lieutenant Schmidt run?
2. What were the names of the two British ships?
3. How much quicker were the British ships in turning?
4. Why was the British Commander bringing his ship to the stern of the 'Louisa'?—"Because there was ——."

1. When did the Commander give the order to stop his ship? When he saw the —— of the 'Louisa'.
2. With what were the men on the 'Louisa' firing?
3. What had the Captain of the 'Louisa' opened?

Chapter **19**

1. Where had the Commander's two reports to be sent?
2. What can Allnutt do?
3. What is a Consul?
4. Where will Rose go?

1. What words settled Rose's future?
2. What did Rose's family always do?
3. What did she say to Allnutt? "We've got to ——."
4. Did they live happily ever after?

LIST OF EXTRA WORDS

anchor 2
awning 2

bellows 8
bend, bent 5
blade 8
boat-hook 3
bow (of a ship) 2

cartridge 15
channel 2
Consul 19
cylinder 2

detonator 2

engine 2

funnel 2

gin 2

handle 3

insect 2

launch 2
leech 11
life-buoy 15

malaria 12
mangrove 12
mission, missionary 1
mud 3

propeller 2
pump 3

reed 10
rifle 18

sea-cocks 18
shaft 8
steer 2
stern 2

tiller 2
torpedo 2

water-lily 11
weld 8

ثروت ہے